Rescue Rover!

Rescue Rover!

101 Ways You Can Help Abandoned Dogs

By
Marie K. Whelan

HOUNDHUT PRESS

Rescue Rover!

Photograph credits:
Cover photo by Dominic Arizona Bonuccelli
Ph: 206-232-8171
Website: http://www.azfoto.com
Author Photo by Glamour Shots

Published by HoundHut Press
For information, please contact:
HoundHut Press
P. O. Box 20062
San Jose, CA 95160-0062
www.houndhut.com
Phone: 408-674-1615

Softback ISBN – 0-9675381-0-6
Hardback ISBN - 0-9675381-1-4

Printed in the United States.

Dedication

To Nora, Conor and Brendan –
You give my life meaning.

To Applejack, Thunder, Dana, Max and Dagmar –
You give my life purpose.

And to God –
You give my life the ability.

Table of Contents

Acknowledgements

This book could not have been written or finished without the enormous contributions of a multitude of people. First, I would like to thank my chief editor and husband, Brendan, for your boundless support and enthusiasum over the years. You believed in me when even I doubted. I will be forever grateful. You are my inspiration.

And to my additional editors, Sheila Whelan, Laura and Robert Engberson and Eugene and Miriam Conser, I owe all of you a mountain of gratitude. Have your people call my people and we'll do lunch :-) I love you.

And finally, to all of the millions of people that selflessly dedicate themselves to dog rescue and placement around the nation. You are my heroes! God bless all of you!

Preface

When I think back to how "Rescue Rover!" came to be, I remember thinking that there must be a positive way to get people involved in dog rescue and place-ment. There already was an over-abundance of sad tales and grim statistics. I thought, "What can one person do to change that dire outcome for thousands of abandoned and endangered dogs?" "Rescue Rover!" became the answer to that question.

The ideas contributed here were culled from hundreds of shelters and placement agencies around the nation. Some of the suggestions may not interest you and some may scream out for you to bring them to life. Feel free to take what you can from this "idea-generat-ing" book and leave the others behind. If you take just one idea from "Rescue Rover!" and use it in your life, you will make a difference in the lives of hundreds of abandoned dogs. *You* have the power to assure that there are no more homeless dogs in America. You <u>can</u> make a difference!

Part 1:

101 Ways You Can Help Abandoned Dogs

1.

Adopt A Rescue Dog

First, let's start with the most basic way to help –
bringing an abandoned dog into your home.

Puppies in most pet stores tug at the heart-strings, but
be aware that there is a thriving puppymill trade that
preys on your sentimental feelings. Hundreds of dogs
are exploited every year to put one cute puppy into pet
stores.

Instead, when you have room in your heart and home
for a four-legged ball of fluff, check out your local
shelter or breed placement group. There are thousands
of dogs with so much love to give who are still in the
prime of their lives.

Decide today to only get a dog from a rescue
organization. It may be only one life you save, but it
will mean the world to that one dog.

2.

Adopt A Shelter or Rescue Group

If you are not ready, or can not adopt a dog, adopt a rescue group. The second best commodity you can give a rescue group (aside from a substantial trust fund) is your TIME. Are you fond of a particular breed? Is there a Humane Society or shelter close to your home? Both breed rescue groups, shelters and local rescue groups are calling out to you. But don't think that if you don't volunteer 5 days a week, the group cannot use you. Any time you can give is of value.

Promise to donate 1 hour a week to helping out a dog rescue group – only ONE HOUR. Keep reading and I'll give you many ideas how you can use that one hour – but right now, commit to yourself to give your time. It is more valuable than you give it credit.

3.

DOG OWNERS
Be a Responsible Pet Owner

If you presently have a dog in your home, you can set an example for others to emulate by being a great owner, and thereby having a super-dog. Make sure you cover the basics of responsible pet ownership for all of your own animals.

- Spay or neuter your pet
- Keep current on all vaccinations
- License your dog with the local authority
- Put a durable collar on your dog with ID licenses and tags
- Keep clear, current pictures of your dogs in case they get lost
- Do not let any animal ride in the back of a pickup truck
- Never leave a pet in a car on a hot day - even for a few minutes, even with the windows cracked open.
- Have your dog examined by your vet every year. You can spot serious health problems early and avoid complications.
- Enroll every puppy immediately into a training class. More than 90% of all surrendered dogs have had no training.

4.

Foster a Dog at Your House

You love dogs and have room at your house…Why not foster a dog until it can be adopted?

Fostering helps dogs in so many ways. Many dogs, straight from abusive or abandoned situations, are quiet and shy. You can get them accustomed to the sound of a friendly voice. You can observe them and determine their compatibility for adoption- Are they good with cats? How about small children? Do they like walks or do they hate the leash? Are they boisterous? Funny? Shy? Playful? Quiet?

When the time comes to interview potential adopters, you can use your experience with the dog to determine an appropriate fit for the dog. This is critical in reducing the number of returns.

Best of all, you get to enjoy them at little or no cost to yourself. Most rescue groups provide the food, supplies and any medical care. All you provide is the home and the love.

5.

NO EXCUSES!
Number 1

Don't accept any excuses dog owners may give you for failing to spay or neuter their dogs.

> Excuse #1 - "I always watch my dog and he will never get any other dog pregnant."

Always? Every moment of the day? Even when you are at work? Even when you are asleep? Is he always securely leashed whenever the door opens? When the garage opens? When the yard fence gate opens?

There are always opportunities for determined, smart and hormonally driven dogs to escape. He isn't deliberately defying you. His hormones take over and he will owe no allegiance to your love. He will only follow the hormonal siren song that has called dogs for centuries. All it takes is a few minutes with a breeding female to create another litter on an already overburdened population.

> If you truly love your dog...neuter him!
> If you truly love your dog...spay her!

6.

Survey Shelters for Pure Breed Dogs for Breed Rescue Groups

Breed rescue groups frequently work with shelters to take possession of a pure breed dog and fosters it. This frees up space in the shelter. The dog will also be exposed and evaluated by people familiar with the breed and may have a better chance to be placed with a family intimately aware of the pros and cons of the breed - and thus a lower chance of return.

You can assist the breed rescue group by helping identify dogs within the shelters that are appropriate to enter the breed foster program. Additionally, if you are able, you can become the shelter's "breed contact" for pickups and transportation of the dogs when they are received.

Contact the breed group, then contact the shelter to begin this kind of communication between the agencies.

7.

FOR YOUTH & TEENS
Boycott Events

So many events that we call "entertainment" can be detrimental to animals such as some circus tours and horse or greyhound racing. If an event comes to your town, don't attend. Be vocal. Write a letter to your TV station and local newspaper. Tell the event coordinator and sponsoring location that you won't attend because it exploits animals. Tell your friends why you choose not to attend these events.

Circus animals are supposedly under the animal welfare act, but it is not always enforced. Unfortunately, some animals are mistreated in these venues and it is difficult to discern whether the laws are followed or not.

Greyhound racing industry looks at dogs as disposable products with 18,000 - 30,000 thrown away and killed every year.

Educate others around you. You can make a difference one voice at a time.

8.

VOTE - Support Animal Rights Legislature

Unfortunately, many Americans have taken for granted our representative government and don't vote or express their opinions to government officials. Exercise your voice in support of the animals.

The easiest way to contribute is to VOTE. Register before your state deadlines and hustle down to your polling place. Investigate the issues on your ballot and vote to support pro-animal rights legislation.

When issues come before your state and county legislature, write, call, email or fax your government officials. Urge them to support pro-animal legislation.

Write to newspapers in support of pro-animal propositions. Be vocal in your support.

Take an active role in your community and world for the benefit of the animals.

9.

USE YOUR SKILLS
Internet Development

Once you have volunteered with a shelter or rescue group, you can use your existing skills to improve the organization.

One of the best ways to increase exposure of the shelter and publicize adoption efforts is to stake out your territory in cyberspace and create a website for your organization. The most basic websites will have address, phone numbers, directions, hours of operation and programs available.

If you have the manpower, put up specific information on the dogs that are available at the shelter. Include their temperament: shy, affectionate, withdrawn or boisterous. What home situation is best for them? Will they need someone home all the time? Are they good with small children? Are they good with other animals such as cats or other dogs? If at all possible include a small picture of them looking their best after a grooming session. Digital photography makes it very easy to get snapshots that are "web-ready".

10.

"Spread the Word"
Talk About Rescue

Encourage adoption of rescued dogs as a great way to share your love. Many people have misconceptions about rescue dogs. They are frequently perceived as "rejected" or "bad" dogs. People think they are all mixed breeds or too old.

Many pure breed puppies and young dogs are abandoned everyday at shelters all across the country. Also, a mixed-breed or older, more mature dog may be more suitable for a person without the patience for a puppy. You can change the misconceptions people have about these fine animals. Go one step further and secure a public venue to talk about dog rescue. Contact your local shelter, rescue group, for additional information to use in your speech.

Possible subjects you can talk about:
- Humane Treatment of Animals
- Shelter Services
- Animal Safety
- Responsible Pet Ownership
- Adopt a Shelter Dog Month (Oct)
- Animal Shelter Appreciation Month (Nov)

11.

Become a Member
of the H.S.U.S.

Founded in 1954, the Humane Society of the United States has consistently been a voice for humane treatment of all animals both wild and domesticated. Their mission is to promote the humane treatment of animals and to foster respect, understanding and compassion for all creatures. They are a nationwide group tackling issues like combating puppy mills, eliminating dog racing and promoting spay and neuter procedures to decrease overpopulation. Education programs run from shelter training to dog bite education. The HSUS even provides disaster relief services.

Minimum membership is a mere $10.00 contribution, but $25.00 or more automatically entitles you to a free one-year subscription to their fine magazine "All Animals". You also receive a membership card, special gifts throughout the year and alerts and updates regarding relevant humane issues.

To join, go to their website at www.hsus.org or write to:
　　　　　The Humane Society of the United States
　　　　　2100 L Street, NW
　　　　　Washington, DC 20037

12.

Office Work

Every organization runs on the efficiency of the office staff and the administration of the needs of that group. Every rescue agency can use extra help in the office.

It doesn't take a Ph.D. to pitch-in and help in the office. Anyone can do letter stuffing or fund-raisers. Simple tasks like data entry are always needed. In cases of emergency, you may be asked to do phone tree calling. But all of these activities are critical in keeping the group running.

So, call your local shelter or rescue group and see if they need help and how you can contribute. For some tasks, you may even be able to take the work home and do it in your own house. But you will still be helping the dogs.

13.

DOG OWNERS
Prepare a "Pet Kit"

If you presently have a dog in your home, proper care of that dog reinforces positive dog ownership and can help reduce the number of dog surrenders to the shelters.

If you live in an area of the country that experiences natural disasters (which can happen just about anywhere), be prepared. Not just for yourself, but for your pets as well. Put together an emergency "pet kit". Here's a list of some of the items to include in your a "pet kit":

- Two-week supply of dry dog food
- Bowls for food and water and a can opener
- Grooming brush and spare towels
- One month supply of any regular medication your pet may need
- Favorite toys
- Dry treats and biscuits
- Leash and collar
- Name and number of your vet, in case you cannot care for your pet
- Up-to-date record of current vaccinations and other medical information

14.

Donate Windfall Money

Sometimes, luck smiles upon you and you may receive a windfall gift. It may be a check from a rebate you forgot you sent in or a gift from a relative for the holidays. Everyone loves finding money in your coat pocket you never knew was there. Why not take a portion of your windfall and give it to the dogs?

It doesn't have to be a cash donation (but those will be accepted). You can go to the local pet store and pick up toys, food, beds or whatever you like. Then drop those off at your local shelter or placement group.

Think of it as a double windfall: one for you and one for the dogs!

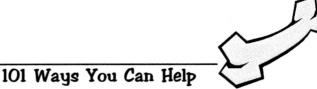

15.

NO EXCUSES!
Number 2

Don't accept any excuses dog owners may give you for failing to spay or neuter their dogs.

Excuse #2 - "My dog will get fat and lazy if I have him neutered."

If the owner feeds the dog a lot of table scraps, then that will be the cause of obesity, not neutering. If a normally active dog is abandoned in the house for days on end when she needs a nightly walk, then that will be the cause of laziness, not spaying. Feeding proper, nutritious dog food and providing ample opportunity for exercise will keep any dog trim, lively and happy. Additionally, the urge to run and fight in a male dog will decline and he will become a better companion as he spends more time with his best friend - YOU!

If you truly love your dog...neuter him!

If you truly love your dog...spay her!

16.

Become a Trainer
FOR FREE!

Once the honeymoon phase of dog purchasing has passed, owners frequently discover dog behaviors that they do not understand and cannot control. Many of these owners abandon their dogs at the shelters. In fact, behavior problems are the number one reason for dog surrender. Among the top problem behavior problems are barking, chewing, hyperactivity, housetraining accidents and aggression toward people and other pets. Many of these can be cured or controlled by understanding dog behavior and by implementing basic training on the dog.

Many humane societies have a goal to provide basic training (sit, down, stay) to their adoptable dogs. These minor training commands truly enhance the control the new owners feel over the dog and reduces the occurrence of re-surrenders.

You can learn how to train dogs - _for free_ - by volunteering to apprentice train at your local humane society. Once you learn the basics, you can train your dog as well! Now you can use this skill to help rescued dogs become obedient and happy members of a new family.

17.

FOR YOUTH & TEENS
Money Makers

Just as with any other group that needs funds, you can organize fund-raisers for your local humane society including one-shot fund-raising events such as car-washes, bake sales, curb painting or spring plant sales. Send some or all of the proceeds to the rescue group.

Dog related jobs, such as grooming, dog-walking or pet sitting can be used to generate revenue for a rescue group.

In fact, any business can enhance their image by following a stated company policy which includes a contribution once-a-year to a shelter or rescue group of a portion of their profits. In that way you can make money for the dogs while making money for your business.

18.

Recruit College Students to Help Volunteer with Dogs

If you are near a college campus, a great source of volunteers can be found in the students of the university. Many students want to volunteer with an animal rescue agency, but since many have relocated from their home for the first time, don't know what groups exist locally and what they can do to help. Once you have volunteered with a rescue organization, you can recruit these students to volunteer with your group.

You can post flyers at local campuses near your organization which includes your group web address and phone number. Redirect that love of animals towards your rescue group and harness the energy of new volunteers.

19.

USE YOUR SKILLS
Maintenance

Do you own a house? Then you probably have experience in maintaining your home. Just as your house needs painting, your local shelter will need painting as well.

Ask about building maintenance projects at your shelter and see if they need community assistance on any projects. They may need help with projects such as weatherproofing for the winter or cleaning up dead branches in the summer. Any of the same tasks you do seasonally at home have to be done at the shelter.

Give them a call and donate a day to beautify your local shelter.

20.

Liquidating Office Furniture?
Donate It!

If your office or business is remodeling the work environment of its employees, find out if the old furniture or office equipment can be donated. Any office items can be used, such as:

- Desks and credenzas
- Bookshelves
- File cabinets
- Office desk and conference room chairs
- Lamps
- Old, operable fax machines
- Stationery supplies

Everything will find a happy new owner at your local shelter. Call ahead to see what they need and when/where to deliver your donation.

In addition, be aware of others who are redecorating their offices or businesses and suggest they send their "desk to the dogs"!

21.

Celebrate National Animal Shelter Appreciation Week

Sponsored by the Humane Society of the United States, National Animal Shelter Appreciation Week typically takes place the 1st full week in November each year. Shelter week was established to thank shelter workers for their tireless dedication, but it also has become a spotlight on the efforts and goals of shelters everywhere.

During this time, make every effort to visit your local shelter. They frequently have special programs and open house tours for visitors to enjoy. Take time to find out about volunteer opportunities at your shelter. Also, spend a moment to thank the shelter workers that are there. A few words of praise and thanks will really make their day!

22.

Teach Children Kindness to Animals

Kindness to all animals begins with the very youngest humanitarians. Teach children to respect dogs and cats as living beings with thoughts and feelings. Show them how to pet a dog with love. And always watch them while they are around dogs as a large or aggressive dog may overwhelm a small child when it wants to play.

While teaching all the good aspects about dogs to children, be aware they need to know that not all dogs are friendly. Be sure they are aware of the warning signs of dog aggression, so an innocent encounter with a stray will not turn into a dog bite.

Check with your local dog trainer and ask if you and a child may simply attend one of their dog training classes. Even if you do not own a dog, it is the perfect opportunity to demonstrate dog behavior to a youngster.

Children always mirror the examples we show them. Let your reflection be one of compassion and education.

23.

DOG OWNERS
Use the Shelter Store

If you are presently have a dog in your home, both of you can benefit dogs that are still in the shelters simply by shopping.

Many shelter locations across the nation include a small store attached to them where you can purchase leashes, cages, food, books, medication, crates – almost anything that any other major chain pet store carries.

A big bonus that sets these stores apart from other retail firms is the fact that a portion of all proceeds are returned to the shelter general fund – enabling the organization to help more animals. Profits generated from retail sales go to facility upkeep, kennel maintenance, adoption staff and services.

If you are going to purchase these supplies anyway, stop by your local shelter store and let your money work twice as hard for the dogs!

For a related tip, see number 62!

24.

What if Your Shelter Doesn't Take Volunteers?

Find out WHY. Keep going up the chain of command until you get a satisfactory answer. It may be because there is not enough paid staff to manage a volunteer program. Or perhaps the facility cannot afford the liability insurance to cover volunteer injuries. Or perhaps there just has never been consistent enough interest in volunteering at the shelter to commit to the program.

Determine if the shelter has an outside volunteer organization that may not work onsite, but does provide fund-raising support for the shelter. These groups are frequently called the "Friends of (the shelter)".

And, if all this fails, ask to meet the director of the shelter personally. Ask how your specific skills and talents may be put to use to benefit the organization.

There are always ways to help out.

25.

NO EXCUSES!
Number 3

Don't accept any excuses dog owners may give you for failing to spay or neuter their dogs.

> Excuse #3 - "I've heard that a female dog should have at least one litter before she should be spayed."

This is simply and "old wives tale". Female dogs do not "miss" the experience of labor and delivery. She will not "forever have an empty spot" because she did not have puppies.

If they use this argument, ask them how empty she will be when they give her children away, because unless the owner wants to raise and feed the puppies, that is exactly what will happen. The owner is anthropomorphizing human emotions onto a dog that will never miss an experience that she does not know exists. In fact, spaying will be even kinder to the dog as she will never suffer the taxing effects of the pregnancy or the discomfort of going into heat.

> If you truly love your dog...neuter him!
> If you truly love your dog...spay her!

26.

Old Toys

Kids tear through toys faster than tissue paper clothing. But discarded toys do not have to clutter your garage. The dogs would love to play with your old, flat tennis balls.

All of the following would make excellent dog toys:
- Old sports balls - basketballs, soccer balls
- Frisbees and throwtoys for active yard play
- Large plastic yard gyms for small dog adventure
- Mini-wading pools for cooling down
- Plastic "play-corral" fencing for containing puppies at adoption fairs

As with all donations, check with your local shelter for needs and delivery hours.

27.

FOR YOUTH & TEENS
Birthdays for the Dogs!

It's your birthday and you just got a beautiful, new rubber squeak toy. Or even better, a fuzzy, stuffed plush that rattles. Sure, maybe that isn't really what you want, but it sure will make some dog's day.

For your next birthday party, request that guests give presents of dog toys or supplies and then donate them to your favorite local group. It's more satisfying knowing that you can have a great party and still help out the pups.

So, next time, let your birthday go to the dogs!

28.

Participate in Meet and Greet Outdoor Events

More and more shelters are leaving the confines of their brick and mortar buildings and bringing their dogs to the adopters at pet store and shopping areas in the community. These events are sometimes called "meet and greets" and you can volunteer at these events.

Volunteer with your local rescue group and coordinate their calendar with yours to determine when they will be conducting a "meet and greet". in your area. Be on hand to help fill out adoption forms, answer rescue group inquiries or assist a dog adopter.

It usually takes 2-4 hours out of your day but will really help the shelter staff.

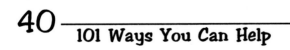

29.

USE YOUR SKILLS
Writing

Shelters and rescue groups are always in need of people with skills in creative writing or editing.

Use your ability to create memorable and inventive advertising to promote the organization. Create and edit articles for the shelter newsletter or for inclusion in the local newspaper. Craft fund-raising letters for direct mail campaigns. Tailor press releases or marketing campaigns for public distribution. Or edit materials submitted by other authors for all of the above activities.

Written materials bring the shelter message to the public. Use your abilities to give that mission life.

30.

Honor Snacks in the Office

Does your office have a coffee or soda area? Stock that area yourself and tell everyone that a portion of the proceeds will go to dog rescue. Coworkers will love to buy snacks knowing that some of their money will go to a good cause.

You can expand this by stocking an honor bar with candy and chips. Ask everyone to use an honor policy for purchases. The dogs will thank your co-workers – and YOU – for thinking of them.

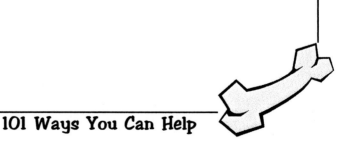

31.

Join the ASPCA

In 1866, Henry Bergh formed a humane organization committed to alleviating pain, fear and suffering in all animals. He called it the American Society for the Prevention of Cruelty to Animals. Since then, the ASPCA has become one of the oldest and largest hands-on animal welfare organizations in the world.

ASPCA contributions fund animal care programs, spay and neuter promotions, behavior and education programs, humane law enforcement and congressional lobbies.

Individual members who pay $20.00 or more a year also receive a subscription to the ASPCA magazine "Animal Watch".

You can contact the ASPCA and join online at their website at:
>   www.aspca.org
or write to them at their national headquarters at:
>   ASPCA
>   424 East 92nd Street
>   New York, NY 10128

32.

Learn Grooming
FOR FREE!

Volunteering at your local shelter can also help you learn a new skill: bathing and grooming dogs.

Most dogs do not look clean and lovely when they are taken off the street and brought to the local shelter. Many are matted, dirty, flea bitten and covered with twigs and grass. The first step to get them presented for adoption is to make them gorgeous, and that means - A BATH!

Check with your local shelter and see if they have a grooming center and determine if they take volunteers that wish to learn grooming. There may be some training and a time commitment required to be a groomer at the shelter, but the knowledge you gain will be worth it. You'll learn humane bathing techniques, including how to calm frightened dogs. Once they are cleaned, then it comes time to trim their coats into appealing cuts.

Before you know it, their shining eyes will now be visible to potential adopters and you can proudly be responsible for their new attractive look.

33.

DOG OWNERS
Share Your Success Story

There are a lot of misconceptions about rescued dogs. People perceive them as rejects and undesirables when in many cases this is patently untrue. If you have been blessed to have a rescued dog under your roof, _tell people about it._

Volunteer at a show and tell day at pet stores. Write a success story article for the rescue organization newsletter where you adopted your beloved buddy. Frequently, they can use them in monthly newsletters or in promotional pieces.

Tell just about everyone who will listen about your tale of rescue success. One at a time, we can dispel this "rescue dog = bad" myth and give every abandoned dog a loving home.

34.

Interview Potential Adopters

In many rescue groups, the key to successful adoption is the owner interview. This is the opportunity to determine the experience and expectations of prospective owners and find an appropriate match from the available dogs. This interview cannot be rushed through or skimmed over without causing undue harm to both sides.

There are many tasks volunteers can do:
- Volunteer to do phone interviews with prospective adopters and find out more about their requirements and capabilities.
- Be the person who performs the home-visit for your area to determine if the home and outdoor areas are appropriate for your specific breed.
- Or follow-up with the new owners and clarify if the adoption is working and clear-up any final questions.

Your breed experience can help new owners bring a new dog into their home and make it a true member of their family.

35.

NO EXCUSES!
Number 4

Don't accept any excuses dog owners may give you for failing to spay or neuter their dogs.

Excuse #4 - "My dogs personality will completely change if I have him neutered."

A dog does not go from happy-go-lucky to vicious simply because he has been neutered. Love, kindness, caring an compassion are the only factors that will determine the emotional outcome of any dog. In male dogs, aggressive and territorial tendencies may even decline after neutering, making the dog more affectionate and agreeable.

If you truly love your dog...neuter him!

If you truly love your dog...spay her!

36.

Webrings

Yahoo! maintains communities of websites that are united by common themes. These are called "webrings" and webmasters can join these webrings by adding their site to the list. One area of webrings is dedicated to various dog breeds. Owners and enthusiasts of various dog breeds that have created websites about their favorite dogs have joined breed specific rings and these are listed at Yahoo!

Viewing these websites can help you understand the reality of owning that breed as well as activities that dog engages in for play.

To find these webrings, go to Yahoo! at:
www.dir.webring.yahoo.com

Dog breeds can be found at www.yahoo.com under:
- Science
  - Biology
    - Animals
      - Mammals
        - Dogs
          - Breeds

37.

FOR YOUTH & TEENS
Sponsor a Pet

Many rescue groups or shelters now allow you to sponsor a pet until it is finally adopted into a loving home. The advantage to this is that you do not physically have to care for the dog, but instead you can contribute financially to the upkeep of the dog while it is in foster care or on-site at the rescue facility.

Another way to generate sponsorship funds is to pool together the resources in your class, school or office place and have a group of friends sponsor a dog.

The financial contribution is a nominal monthly fee (usually $25-$50 a month) and is tax-deductible if donated to a nonprofit group.

Contact a rescue group or shelter in your area and ask if they have a pet sponsorship program.

38.

Media Contact

Do you have contacts at local TV or radio stations?
Do you know a columnist at the local newspaper?
You can become the media liaison for your rescue
group.

Take your shelter activity calendar and make sure the
"about town" section adds it to their listing. Provide
contact names to TV or radio stations so if an issue
comes up surrounding dogs, your organization can be
contacted for comments. Keep your shelter or rescue
group name in the public eye. Someday, one of those
readers will need you and know how to get in touch
with your group - all because of your consistent public
presence.

39.

USE YOUR SKILLS
Drawing/Artwork

If you can sketch, draw, color or layout posters, flyers or advertising - you are needed at your local rescue organization. Creative ability is useful in the creation of memorable and professional advertising and marketing campaigns. Designing posters for events or seminars publicizes organization activities. And simple items, such as flyers, brochures and handouts all need to be designed before they can be printed for distribution.

So whether you are a professional graphics illustrator or an amateur artist, grab your pencils and paper and head on down to the shelter or rescue group. You can draw the way to a better and brighter future for the dogs.

40.

Employer Matching Donations

You can effortlessly double any cash donation you provide the shelter without draining your pocketbook - just ask your boss!

A lot of people are unaware of this benefit, but many employers in the US offer matching donations to 501(c)(3) or other non-profit agencies. Those that don't match dollar for dollar may offer $.50 or $.25 to every dollar donated by an employee. Some companies only offer this benefit during charitable drives for payroll deductions or United Way drives.

So check with your Human Resources department on their policy regarding nonprofit organization donations. If all it takes is to fill out one form to double your donation, won't you do that for the dogs?

41.

Check AKC Breed Rescue

The American Kennel Club maintains lists of club web pages (see "Section 3: AKC Breed Groups and Websites"). They also keep names and phone numbers of individuals within their clubs that specialize in pure breed rescue. Most have a single contact, but some clubs have designated regional contacts which will assist you in locating rescue dogs closer to you. These are completely different from the breeder contacts which are also listed on the AKC website.

Rescue representatives may have dogs surrendered to them from former owners, kennels, breeders that do not want to breed a specific dog for whatever reason, or simply abandoned dogs referred to the club.

These dogs are mostly 100% purebred dogs because that is what AKC primarily handles. You can find these contacts at the AKC website at:
www.akc.org/breeds/rescue.cfn

42.

Flea Market Finds

Next time you visit a flea market, garage sale, yard sale or a tag sale, think about your local shelter or rescue group.

Not only is any pet supply of value at the shelter, but old, functional office supplies, towels and linens - even tools and other maintenance supplies can be used at a rescue organization.

Contact your local rescue group, shelter or humane society for their "wish lists" of donations they are seeking. Check their website where their wish lists are frequently posted. You can get some ideas of items that can be useful at the shelter in the appendix "Section 2: Wish Lists" at the back of this book. If you find a good value at the garage sales, it could pay off for the shelter and you in a tax-deductible donation.

43.

DOG OWNERS
Donate Used Pet Supplies

Do you have any toys that your dog never used? Are there coats your dog outgrew? Do you have any supplies that your dog simply did not like? If so, donate them to your local shelter.

Half used bottles of shampoo can still make a dirty rescue as clean as a show dog. Old metal bowls, brushes, balls, kennels and crates can have a second life.

Check with your local humane society or rescue group to find out their specific needs. Check the back of this book under "Section 2: Wish Lists" for a list of some supplies a group may need.

44.

Get Moving!

Running errands all over town? Can't spend time volunteering at the shelter office? Consider including errands for a shelter along with your own tasks.

Rescue groups need people to provide transportation to complete the many projects at the shelter. The following are some examples of the tasks where rescue groups need transportation:

· You can pickup donations at drop off sites and bring them to the shelter.

· Bring dogs to and from the vet.

· Drop off weekly pet supplies to foster homes in your area.

Check the rescue group, shelter or humane society for transportation needs in your area.

45.

NO EXCUSES!
Number 5

Don't accept any excuses dog owners may give you for failing to spay or neuter their dogs.

Excuse #5 - "I just can't castrate my boy."

I am amazed how often this excuse comes up and how utterly unsubstantiated it is. A dog does not feel "different" or "emasculated" after neutering. Any undue attention or licking the dog may pay to his testicular area may just be due to itching or naturally healing of the surgical site. It is <u>not</u> because the dog feels castrated. This is the owner simply transferring their human emotions onto their dogs that simply are not there.

If you truly love your dog...neuter him!

If you truly love your dog...spay her!

46.

Grocery Store Programs

In some areas of the country, grocery stores run programs which offer rebates to nonprofit organizations. These usually take one of several forms:

1. Receipt programs where you save receipts and turn them in to the shelter so that they may earn the rebate.

2. A scan card program - At the check out in the store, you use a credit card sized scan card to credit a portion of your total purchase to the shelter. (The shelter must be registered for this program with the vendor ahead of time.)

Contact your local shelter or rescue group to determine if they are enrolled in these or similar kinds of programs.

47.

FOR YOUTH & TEENS
Gardening

If you mow lawns for neighbors, take 10-20% of any earnings you make and set it aside for the pups. At the end of the season, you can either donate the cash or purchase an item the group needs and bring it to them.

Adults can also expand on this concept by donating as well - and saving money in the process. If you pay a gardener to mow your lawn, do it yourself once a month and give the gardener the weekend off. Take the money you would have spent on the gardener and send it to the shelter.

Expand upon the concept when doing the same tasks for :
- · Raking leaves
- · Shoveling snow
- · Performing oil changes
- · Washing cars

48.

Encourage "Baby-proofing"

Many people surrender dogs after a new baby arrives simply because they haven't babyproofed the dog. If you are expecting a baby or know someone who is, encourage babyproofing the dog to create a seamless merger of the new arrival into the dogs world.

Babyproofing a dog consists of slowly bringing baby items into the dogs world so that the actual arrival of the baby isn't threatening to the dog. First, gradually reduce one-on-one time with the dog to have smaller moments of quality time. Don't suddenly decrease attention to the dog after the baby arrives or the dog will have negative associations with the baby and feel threatened.

Then introduce the dog to baby items and let him investigate these new items.

Lastly, bring a blanket home from the hospital early with the baby's scent on it. Remember, it is not the baby that will upset the dog, it is the change in his routine. Make changes slowly and the dog and the baby will merge together flawlessly.

49.

USE YOUR SKILLS
Photography/Videography

Here's a great idea that is frequently in high demand at shelters and placement groups. If you can take a still picture without cutting heads off or you can film and edit videotape, you are in demand.

Printed brochures and newsletters always look better with photos. It adds a more personal touch and the reader can visualize the subject. Additionally, many groups are now using the internet to post pictures of adoptable dogs. One afternoon of snapping photos can satisfy both of these needs.

Video experience can always be used to make short films and promotional pieces. Computer capabilities would help with scanning, editing and distribution of advertisements or educational material.

Call your local group to help.

50.

Donate Professional Skills

No matter what you do for a living, you can give your time, donating that exact skill, to the shelter. Here's an example of some wide ranging professions where the skills they have can still be used by rescue groups.

- Accountants and attorneys can provide consulting on issues of finance or legality to the shelter.

- Massage therapists can aide wounded dogs recovering from surgery.

- Psychologists can review applicants for appropriate fit between the owners and the new dog.

- Nurses can aide in administering first shots to puppies.

- Cab drivers can transport critical supplies and food to foster homes.

Everyone is needed at the shelter.

51.

Join Best Friends Animal Sanctuary

At any given time up to 1800 abandoned dogs, cats, horses and other animals live on 350 acres in Southern Utah at Best Friends Animal Sanctuary. There they have reached a no-kill sanctuary of veterinary care, compassion and happy people. They wait safely for the day they can be adopted or live out their lives at this sanctuary.

The mission of Best Friends is to "help bring about a time when there are no more homeless pets and when every cat or dog who's ever been born can be guaranteed a good home with a loving family."

Additionally, they sponsor the Best Friends Network (see number 71), spay/neuter clinics, hands-on seminars to learn how to rescue animals and start an animal sanctuary and provide mobile adoption, fostering and education programs.

You can reach them at their website at:
www.bestfriends.org
or write to them at: Best Friends Animal Sanctuary
5001 Angel Canyon Road
Kanab, UT 84741-5001

52.

Puppy Needs

Puppies tend to get abandoned at the shelters without their mother and therefore require more specialized care than most adult dogs.

They need more nutrients and have more sensitive digestions than older dogs. When those puppies are separated from their mother and need nutrition, Esbilac puppy formula fits that bill. Esbilac can be picked up at your local pet store and it stores well for use at the shelter.

You can also donate old hot water bottles to simulate the warmth of a mother. Old towels can provide soft comfort to a frightened pup. Simple items like eyedropper can be used to feed the puppies formula.

Contact your local rescue group or shelter for specific needs.

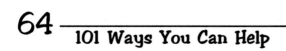

53.

DOG OWNERS
Prepare for a Lost Dog

Many dogs end up in shelter because they run away and become lost. If you own a dog, it is critical that you know what to do if your dog is lost to prevent your dog from becoming part of the statistics.

First determine when the dog escaped. This could help determine how far away from home he could have run. Check the neighborhood, walk slowly and call out the dog's name and shake a box of treats or jingle car keys if that will attract the dog's attention. Inform as many people as possible about the dog's breed, color, collar, tags, distinguishing features. If possible, bring a picture.

Create a flyer with the dogs name, description and a contact name and phone number. Include a "reward" if you can, but pay it only after you and your pet have been reunited.

Check if your community has a business that specialized in finding lost pets. Visit your local shelters daily. Go through their "found" lists. Check "found animals" in the paper and place a "lost dog" ad. Keep looking and keep your spirits up.

54.

What Do Shelters Want?

There are many volunteer positions available at your local shelter and placement groups. The following is a partial list of potential positions. If your local organization does not have this position formally recognized and you think you would be great in this job, suggest it to the board. They would love your enthusiasm. And don't believe you can only be of value if you can give 20-40 hours a week. Any amount of time is needed.

· Adoptions Counselor
· Greeter
· Language translator/interpreter
· Dog Walker
· Grooming and Bathing
· Obedience Training
· Socializer
· Feeding
· Puppy and Dog Fostering
· Humane Education Teacher
· Off-Site Adoption Worker
· Event marketing and promotions worker
· Food/Animal pickup transportation
· Fund-raising
· Outreach clinic worker

55.

NO EXCUSES!
Number 6

Don't accept any excuses dog owners may give you for failing to spay or neuter their dogs.

> Excuse #6 - "I want my kids to view the miracle of birth."

A dog may have 10 puppies in a litter, each of which will be able to breed in a year, having the potential of 10 puppies each themselves. And so on, and so on. In 5 years, one unaltered dog can be responsible for 100,000 dogs thrust upon and overcrowded and overburdened society. Unless that owner and their family can support that many dogs, then rent a video to "witness the miracle of birth" or buy a book. Society can't handle this "miracle of birth".

> If you truly love your dog...neuter him!

> If you truly love your dog...spay her!

56.

Recycle Your Remodel

Have you just finished remodeling a room? Have you made some construction changes to your house? Do you have any leftover construction supplies taking up space in your garage? Donate them to your local shelter.

Every rescue facility has something in need of repair. They can use just about every construction supply: plumbing, insulation, nails, drywall, screws, plywood, paints, caulks or whatever you can provide.

Be sure to call the organization ahead of time to determine what supplies they can use and when to drop them off. Some facilities may have offsite drop-off areas or even a gate at the opposite end of the main entrance. If one organization cannot use your supplies at this time, call another. Be sure to get a receipt so you can deduct the fair-market value of the goods on your taxes for the year.

57.

FOR YOUTH & TEENS
Flower Sales from Seed

Do you have a green thumb? An easy way to combine your gardening skills with your love of dogs is to have a plant sale.

Every spring, people strike out in hopes of finding good quality vegetable and flower seedlings to decorate their yards. You can inexpensively plant a variety of seeds, and with little maintenance, grow them to seedlings that can be sold at 10-100 times the per seed cost.

Create a greater incentive for your buyers to purchase from you by saying a portion (or all) of your profits are being donated to dog rescue. You can also sell your plants via the group directly to attach the group's name in a more meaningful way. It is more satisfying to buy your plants and know you are helping charity rather than a corporate bottom line.

58.

Distribute Flyers

Are you located far away from your local humane society or are you located in an area not immediately serviced by your rescue group? You can still help out even if you visit the rescue headquarters once a month.

Volunteer to pick up brochures from your rescue group once a month and then distribute the flyers or information brochures to pet stores, groomers and veterinarians in your area. If your organization does not have an established relationship with these businesses, you can become the local liaison. Once this relationship has been established, you can replenish the promotional material once a month, and still stay in your area.

59.

USE YOUR SKILLS
Gardening

Like a home, a shelter can look more beautiful with a touch of greenery throughout, but the foliage needs to be planned, planted and maintained. If you have a green thumb, you can certainly help out.

Find out if your local shelter needs landscaping or interior houseplants for decor. Offer to start flowerboxes at windows. Plant half-barrel planters with shrubs, seasonal flowers and ivy. Take cuttings from your houseplants and create beautiful indoor greenery for shelter offices. Or perhaps you can grow small containers of catnip or grass for sale in the society giftshop.

Contact your local shelter director for information on how your gardening skills can make their buildings beautiful.

60.

Give a Speech for the Dogs

If you are a member of a social organization, or if you are a public speaker, you can use any of your public speaking engagements to benefit the dogs.

Simply state that the proceeds will be earmarked for your local humane or rescue organization. Or, if you are not being paid for speaking, ask attendees to bring one can of dog food or a dog toy to the event. Be sure to announce that these donations will go to the rescue group.

Publicize the event through your local paper. Many papers will list events at no charge and provide free publicity. Additionally, copy flyers and distribute them to local businesses that would be interested in your topic.

A special touch would be to invite a representative of the pet organization to the event. At some point, he or she can briefly describe the organization and generate more exposure.

61.

Shelters Should Join "Shelter Partners"

After you join a shelter or rescue group, encourage them to become a member of "Shelter Partners." All private or public shelters are all able to join this new program started by the Humane Society of the United States.

All it takes is to fill out a 15 minute application and return it to the HSUS. The shelter then becomes part of a community where multiple shelters are joined to create a stronger force which receives benefits from big firms. The HSUS negotiates with firms, backed by the support of all of the enrolled shelters, to receive discounts, income-generating programs and other cost saving benefits for shelters.

To become a part of this program, contact the HSUS at:
> The Humane Society of the United States
> 2100 L Street NW
> Washington, DC 20037
> shelterpartners@hsus.org

62.

Humane "Thrift Shops"

Some humane societies supplement donations by running ancillary stores, such as thrift shops, in conjunction with their humane activities.

If you need to shop at thrift stores, frequent the ones that benefit humane groups. If you are making a donation of clothing, bedding or other household items, consider allowing them to be resold in the Humane Thrift shop. You can clean out your house, redesign or redecorate your personal space while helping out the dogs at the same time.

For a related tip, see number 23!

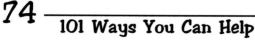

63.

DOG OWNERS
What if You Become Ill?

Are you presently a dog owner? Suppose you are incapacitated in an accident and can no longer care for your dog, either in the short term or long term. Do you know what will happen to your dog? You should. If you do not provide for your dogs, they may end up as surrendered animals in the shelter if something should happen to you.

Think about it now. If you were not available to provide care for your animals, who would be able to take care of them? A relative? A friend? Discuss that with them and get it in writing.

Check with your local shelter or rescue group. Many of them have programs to assist people who become ill and cannot care for their pet. Find out how to activate this service if you become incapacitated.

64.

Volunteer to Work With Youth

If you can touch the minds of the youth, you can touch the future. Youth organizations are always looking for volunteer speakers to instruct classes and you can use these lectures as opportunities to teach humane treatment of animals.

Ask local boy or girl scout troops if they need a speaker to discuss rescue opportunities. Does the youth group for a local church or synagogue need a service project? How about a shelter cleanup? Can an afterschool group promote a fund-raising campaign? How about bringing shelter dogs to a summer camp for a bathing and grooming demonstration?

You can be the person that first exposes these young children to the challenges - and ultimate satisfaction - of dog rescue and proper placement into a good home.

65.

NO EXCUSES!
Number 7

Don't accept any excuses dog owners may give you for not spaying or neutering their dogs.

> Excuse #7 - "I'm a responsible owner. I will always find homes for the puppies."

Do they fully investigate every prospective owner who purchases a puppy? Do they conduct a house visit before releasing the puppy? Do they follow-up with calls and/or visits after the new owner leaves with the puppy? If not, then they are not being a responsible owner.

And what about the puppies available in shelters? An equal number of puppies will have to be put down because their prospective homes have been taken by these other puppies.

There are more than enough puppies available in shelters. New ones are not needed.

If you truly love your dog...neuter him!
If you truly love your dog...spay her!

66.

Overnight Fostering

In rescue situations, sometimes a long term foster stay is not always required by a foster home. If you are not available for long term foster care, volunteer to be a foster caregiver for emergency or transport situations.

If a rescue has come up suddenly, the long term foster home may not be ready to accept the dog. If you can foster it overnight until the long-term home is ready, your could really help out in a time of need.

Additionally, if the rescue group is moving a dog between foster homes or from a foster to a new owner, there may be a need for you to hold the dog for one night. If you can handle that one night rather than long-term, you may be able to satisfy your need to help without the long term foster commitment.

67.

FOR YOUTH & TEENS
"THON" It!

Many organizations run fund-raisers throughout the year in the form of "thon"s.
- Walk-A-Thons
- Run-A-Thons
- Bike-A-Thons
- Pool-A-Thons
- Bowl-A-Thons
- Dog-Walk-A-Thons

Thons abound around us. Contact your local humane group and see if they have any fund-raising events you can participate in. Many walks and runs can also involve your dog trekking with you.

If you work with a group, see if you can coordinate a thon for your organization. Offer prizes for top donations, fastest speed, costumes - whatever! It may take some time, but the results can be fun!

68.

Large Donations

A short while ago, I had a van that was in great shape for a fourteen-year old vehicle. The interior was great with no tears and minimal wear. The engine was solid and it easily had another 50,000 miles to give. When I needed to trade-up to a larger van, what did I do? I donated the van to a greyhound rescue group.

Shelters and rescue groups can frequently handle larger donations and still provide a tax write-off for the donor. Perhaps you have a car that won't run or an old, rusty truck. Maybe you have a boat that will require more work than you want to put into it or even a motorcycle gathering dust. Any property, stocks, bonds or lots of real estate can be donated, for a tax deduction, to a shelter. Contact your local shelter for vehicle donation programs available.

What happened to that van I donated? The rescue group sold it to another member of the rescue group who needed an inexpensive van for her aging greyhounds with her full purchase price went to the greyhound group as a donation. It makes me feel good to know that van is still helping rescued dogs

69.

USE YOUR SKILLS
Sewing

If you can thread a needle, your skills are in demand.
Rescue groups willingly accept creations you can pull
together. Here are some great ideas of items you can
create to be used in the shelter store or at a fund-raising
event:

- · Dog beds
- · Dog Coats and rain slickers
- · Plush toys
- · Blankets
- · Monogrammed Towels
- · Aprons and Oilcloth grooming smocks
- · lab coats

All kinds of dog treats can be made using scraps of
fabric and your talent.

70.

Create a Website for Your Group

The internet can bring your rescue group or organization right into the homes of adoptive families and donors. Even people with minimal skills can use programs provided from ISP (internet service providers) to create professional websites to showcase your group. For a nominal one time investment, you can purchase website software to create sites as well.

Any 501(c)(3) nonprofit rescue, shelter or humane society can get free website hosting from www.dog.com.

If your organization can take digital photographs of adoptable animals, they can also be listed on the web where they can be viewed by the public.

Additionally, an internet directories for homeless and adoptable pets can be found at www.petfinder.com or www.petshelter.org.

71.

Support the
"Best Friends Network"

Best Friends Network is set up by the Best Friends Animal Sanctuary in Kanab, UT. If you are interested and able to help out with emergency rescue situations in your area, sign up at the Best Friends website (www.bestfriends.org). Whenever a rescue issue arises in your area, the network activates and sends emails to everyone signed up in that region. These issues can range from the closing of a shelter looking for permanent or temporary foster homes to a single person needing help with the safe capture of a stray animal that could be wounded.

If you can volunteer professional services, from legal to grooming, sign up with the network to be informed if your skills are ever needed. Additionally, rescue groups and humane societies can sign up to alert individuals of their needs. Or, if you just want to communicate or meet with others who have the desire to contribute to pet rescue, the network can help you "link-up" with all of these people.

72.

Cover It Up!

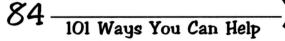

When you are dealing with lots of dogs every day, as many shelter workers do, you discover how easily your clothing attracts pet hair.

If you have anything to cover up your clothes, consider donating it. Items like the following are always in need:

- Old Aprons
- Lab Coats
- Windbreakers
- Medical Scrubs

Help make hard working shelter workers a little cleaner.

73.

DOG OWNERS
Recover from Pet Loss

Have you recently lost a dog? For dog owners, even the mere thought of losing their dear friend can bring them to tears. When I lost my dog, I was devastated. No amount of tears eased my loss. But in the midst of my mourning, I went to the shelter and found hope.

Looking up at me were more dogs that needed the love and caring I wanted to give. I stayed with them, petting and talking with them, and in the end, it helped us both. By spending this time at the shelter after my dogs death, I helped myself heal and the dogs at the shelter become familiar with the love and affection of people.

Inquire with your local shelter. Many have established grief support counselors or grief support groups to help those that have lost their four-footed friend. Also, check out www.petloss.com for online support.

Take the time you need to grieve. Don't feel pressured to rush through it. It may help to remember that there are more dogs out there that need and want your love.

74.

"In Memory of" or
"In Honor Of" Donations

Do you know someone who loves dogs as if they were children? Was there a particular dog that touched your life and that you will always remember? These are great examples of reasons to donate to shelters "In honor of" and "In memory of" that person or animal.

Most rescue organizations accept donations made by you to commemorate someone else. In some instances, these people can be recognized in the shelter newsletter in a special section dedicated to "In honor of" and "In memory of" donation.

You can even ask that people donate to these organizations in lieu of giving you gifts for an occasion in your life such as birthdays, anniversaries, holidays, etc., using the "In honor of" program.

Check with your local shelter to determine if they manage this type of donation service.

75.

NO EXCUSES!
Number 8

Don't accept any excuses dog owners may give you for failing to spay or neuter their dogs.

> Excuse #8 - "My dog is very sensitive and spaying is painful. Besides, that Elizabethan collar is inhumane."

Both spaying and neutering procedures are performed under anesthesia and are painless to the dog. Any discomfort from the stitches are minor and Elizabethan collars are used to prevent the dog from chewing the stitches and causing an infection. It isn't meant to be glamorous, but it does its job with minimal discomfort to the dog.

Failing to spay or neuter a pet can cause more painful complications later on. And altering your dog has the added advantage of reducing or even removing the possibility for cancer of the testes or prostate in male dogs and uterine or breast cancer in the females.

> If you truly love your dog...neuter him!
> If you truly love your dog...spay her!

76.

Try Out a Breed by Fostering Before You Adopt

Have you always dreamed of having a German Shepherd? Did you always want a Yorkie? Find out if that breed is right for you by volunteering to foster. Discover before you adopt that Alaskan Malamute fur stands out against your black couch. Find a match to your personality ahead of time.

Contact any of the breed rescue groups located in the appendices of this book and they will put you in contact with the local rescue group. The local group will interview you and may have a coordinator visit your house to help you prepare for fostering. In most cases, the group picks up all food and medical costs while you provide the love.

The worst that can happen is that you discover the breed you always wanted isn't as much of a match as you once thought. The best that can happen is you fall in love with your foster dog and adopt him yourself.

77.

FOR YOUTH & TEENS
Pennies for Puppies

"Have-a-penny, leave-a-penny" We have all seen these little bowls or cups in stores everywhere. But what about at your office or in your home? What do you do with all your pennies? How about creating a "Pennies for Puppies" jar and leaving all your pennies there? You'll lighten up that change load in your purse and eliminate that jangle in your pocket as you walk.

Or, become more ambitious and expand your collection efforts to "Dollars for Doggies," "Fifties for Fido," "Hundreds for the Hounds," or just "Money for Mutts." They will always happily take whatever donation you can give.

78.

Donate "One"

The contribution of "one" can really make a difference for rescue groups. But one "what" you may ask? One anything!

· Donate one hour a week to stuff envelopes

· Donate one week a month to train dogs

· Donate one month a year to foster dogs

If you think that you don't have the time, realize the larger picture of your contribution. You are giving up a small fraction of your time out of the 365 days in a year to help the dogs – a cause that is important to you. You can do it!

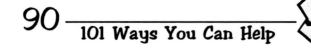

79.

USE YOUR SKILLS
Shelter Repair

In every shelter, something is in disrepair. Maybe the washer is temperamental. Perhaps an outlet doesn't deliver electricity. It could be anything.

If you have certified experience in electrical, plumbing, HVAC or any other technical skill, the shelter needs you!

If you can spare one day a month, only twelve times a year, dedicate that day to repairing areas of the shelter.

Contact the shelter manager to volunteer.

80.

Underage Fostering

Puppies under the age of eight weeks are considered unavailable for adoption and in some states it is illegal to adopt animals before this time. However, these little ones are left at shelter doorsteps every day. They take more "hands-on" care than the shelter has time to provide.

You can foster these pups until they become old enough to adopt. They usually require specialized care and regular feedings, but your hard work will pay off in puppy kisses.

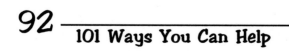

81.

Support
"No More Homeless Pets"

"No More Homeless Pets" is a campaign to eliminate euthanasia of unwanted pets through education and community support. It is sponsored by Best Friends Animal Sanctuary and supported by hundreds of rescue and humane groups across the nation.

There are many way to support this cause, primarily by endorsing "no-kill" groups in your area and by participating in spay and neuter campaigns, Here are other ways to support the "No More Homeless Pets" campaign:

- Help your local rescue group find good homes for dogs.
- Organize "Spay Day" programs.
- Encourage your community to become an example of humane activity.

For more information, check out
"www.bestfriends.org"

82.

Old Baby Supplies

Once the baby has grown up, you'll have many things you no longer need.

Leftover shampoos can be donated to bathe dogs and puppies. Old baby bottles with nipples don't have to be tossed to the garbage. They can feed puppies that are dependent on formula feedings. Utensils to puree food can ease an abandoned pup into solid foods. Baby towels, burp rags and blankets can be used for bedding. Here's a great idea for all of those cloth diapers. They make great cleanup towels for kennels and are soft enough for eye and ear cleaning while grooming.

When your kids get older, don't send those old baby items to a landfill – donate'em!

83.

DOG OWNERS
Be Prepared for Disaster

Flood, fire, earthquake, tornado, hurricane, power loss, severe weather; all of these can create a situation where we are forced to leave our homes for a period of time. Spend a little time now preparing a disaster plan that includes provisions for your pets.

- Prepare a "pet kit" (see idea 13) that you can grab in an emergency.
- Determine a list of friends and family that could house your animals. Multiple pets may be more comfortable kept together.
- Contact hotels outside your immediate area. Determine which ones allow pets. Are there limits to quantity and size? Will they waive "no pets" in times of emergency?
- Create a list of kennels or vets that provide boarding services in an emergency. Be aware that in a disaster situation, humane societies may already be overburdened.
- Make copies of your dog's vaccination and medical records in case you need to board. They will need this information and you may not be able to make copies when you need them.

84.

Encourage Your Local Shelter to Become "No Kill"

Humane groups all over America are discovering the benefits of becoming a no-kill shelter. In 1987, 17 million dogs and cats were destroyed in shelters across the United States. Estimated now reduce that number from 5-12 million. Unfortunately, that is still 5-12 million too many.

Encourage your local shelter to become no-kill. Support groups that are no-kill. Donate to support "no kill" options.

Use your voice. Speak out against euthanasia for unwanted dogs. Join the "no kill" cause and campaign to eliminate killing animals except in medical necessity.

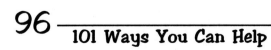

85.

NO EXCUSES!
Number 9

Don't accept any excuses dog owners may give you for failing to spay or neuter their dogs.

> Excuse #9 - "If he was meant to be neutered, he would have been born that way. Neutering a dog just isn't natural."

Do you see hundreds of different breeds of giraffes? How about squirrels? Skunks? No, there may be 2 or 3 varieties, but certainly not hundreds. That is what nature creates. But there are hundreds of types of dogs all over the world. They are bred for herding, racing or leisure. The minute mankind began consciously selecting and breeding certain dogs to create dominant features, dogs lost that "natural" evolution.

What should be natural is humane treatment of all dogs. That means providing for all dogs and limiting their population because there aren't enough homes for them all.

> If you truly love your dog...neuter him!
> If you truly love your dog...spay her!

86.

Kennels, Cages and Crates

I did it too. I admit it. I bought this beautiful crate for my dog. It was solid, durable and easy to use. I was told he would love to have a space to call his own. He would repeatedly retreat to his crate as a source of comfort. Yeah, right.

Years later, my beloved hound sleeps on our couch and has his comfy foam bed. He looks at his crate with disgust as it sits, unused, wasting space in my garage. So, I donated it!

Now, some dogs really do benefit from crate training. It keeps them calm and offers them reassurance of their "own space." However, my dog did not need his crate. But the rescue groups did.

They can use them for crate-trained dogs and for vehicle transportation of fostered animals. They use them in any size and I now have space in my garage.

87.

FOR YOUTH & TEENS
"Love in a Can"

You've seen the donation cans everywhere, but how do they get there? Once you are involved with a humane group or rescue organization, determine if these donation cans can be of benefit to your group.

A person must take responsibility for talking to the local stores and getting permission to leave the cans. Be sure the contents cannot be easily accessed by anybody. A narrow neck bottle or a wide neck jar with a securely sealed lid will work well. Decorate the can with your group or organization name, address and phone number.

Determine what stores will take the cans and how many they need. Can you leave pamphlets there or only the can?

Visit these stores weekly or monthly to collect any money and send it to the treasurer. Inspect the cans for tampering and restock flyers or brochures. Don't forget to thank the store and acknowledge their commitment to your cause after the fund-raising is completed.

88.

Speak for the Dogs

It's summertime and the fleas are jumpin'. Do you know a vet willing to take the time to speak about the latest in flea prevention in dogs? If so, see if you can arrange an event where the vet can speak and donate the proceeds.

Just about any animal specialist can present a topic. All that is needed is a speaker with knowledge about dog issues and a captive audience, which you provide.

- How about a nail trimming clinic from a groomer?

- A technician can speak about heartworm prevention and treatment.

- A kennel owner can speak about vacation preparation to reduce the stress to your favorite pooch?

The possibilities are endless…

89.

USE YOUR SKILLS
Bookkeeping

Do you have a flair for financial matters? Does your checkbook balance with every statement? If so, you can use these skills to help by volunteering to keep bookkeeping for a small rescue group. This may take a little research on nonprofit groups, but it will be worth it.

A rescue group can only be run if it has the resources. You can keep the group on track!

90.

Inexpensive Supplies

If you work for a rescue group or want to donate to them, check out your local Salvation Army or Goodwill for supplies. Kitchen appliances are dramatically discounted. Towels and linens can be used for bedding and grooming.

Check out your local shelter's wish list and feel good shopping for the dogs while a part of your money goes back to your community.

91.

Shop Cruelty-Free

Some dogs are sold to labs that continue to test consumer products on them to determine if humans will have a similar reaction. These tests may cause, at a minimum discomfort, but at the worst, death. Animal testing is inhumane and many animals are tortured. These wonderful, social animals live their lives in cages, terrified, helpless and in pain day after day. That is NO way to treat "man's best friend."

However, some companies have taken a stand against this method and have refused to test on animals. Others have also gone further and also banned any animal ingredient from their product. You can help stop the suffering of these animals by purchasing products from these companies.

A list of these companies can be found in a book titled: "Shopping Guide for Caring and
Compassionate Consumers - A guide to
products that are not tested on animals"
It is updated every year and can be purchased at bookstores or online at www.amazon.com and
www.peta.org.

92.

Be a Hero

If you suspect that any dog is a victim of abuse or neglect, report it to your local humane society or other appropriate agency immediately.

The eyes for these agencies cannot be everywhere. Your diligence will pay off for these animals. Additionally, each report can build up and be used to prosecute humane treatment violators in court.

Animal cruelty is now a felony in 27 states. Work to toughen the laws in your area. Write letters to prosecutors, judges and others involved in the legislative process.

Also, if you see a stray, notify these agencies for pickup. A dog is much more vulnerable to vehicles and uncaring people in the outdoors than in a shelter.

Phone numbers for stray animal pickup and abuse violations can usually be found in the white pages of your local phonebook. Or contact your local humane society for information.

93.

DOG OWNERS
Train for Pet Therapy

If your dog is a calming influence on your life, consider sharing that feeling. Get in touch with a "pet touch therapy" group in your area. You and your dog can visit the elderly and infirmed, offering happiness and cuddling.

Humane societies frequently affiliate adoptees with Pet Therapy, also known as Animal Assisted Therapy or AAT. It is a great tool to help improve the health and well-being of patients in hospitals, nursing homes and other personal care facilities by bringing dogs to them for visitation. There is documented proof that simply petting a dog lowers blood pressure, slows the heart rate and reduces stress levels. Pet therapy is incredibly beneficial to patient, animal and owner.

There are many fine organizations and books available to determine if you and your pet are appropriate for AAT. The application process is comprehensive, just to get a feel for where you and your dog will fit in best, but you'll be happy with the results. Contact your local humane society for agencies in your area that specialize in Pet Therapy.

94.

Wills

Smart life planning includes preparing for your own death and ensuring you have left a will. In this final gesture, you can still create a gift for the dogs in your local shelter.

You can bequeath a memorial donation to be left in your name from funds you will leave behind. Additionally, you can leave items - cars, jewelry or property - to the rescue group.

As you are tying up your personal issues, do not forget about caring for any pets you may leave behind. Designate someone to become a custodian for your dog(s) after you are gone and make sure that person is willing to become their caretaker.

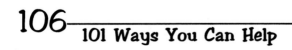

95.

NO EXCUSES!
Number 10

Don't accept any excuses dog owners may give you for failing to spay or neuter their dogs.

> Excuse #10 - "Fifi is such a cute dog.
> I want lots more just like her."

Breeding a dog does not assure that the offspring will be just like the mother or the father. Each dog is unique and different and will never be exactly like either parent, regardless of the owners intentions.

Tell that person to go to the surrendered animals area of their local shelter. There they will find lots of "special" and "cute" dogs and each is looking for a home. They don't need to be put down simply because their homes were taken by another litter, namely "fifi's puppies".

> If you truly love your dog...neuter him!

> If you truly love your dog...spay her!

96.

Perform a 30-Minute Rescue

A 30-minute rescue requires you to donate 30 minutes of your time to make a real difference with a shelter dog.

After you have formally signed up as a volunteer with your local shelter, determine when you can do a 30-minute rescue. You can choose from many different projects to do with one of the shelter dogs. If you are proficient in grooming, use your 30-minute rescue to bathe and trim a recent arrival at the shelter. If your experience is with instruction, you can assist in training a dog in the basic tasks - sit, lay, stay. Or just take your 30-minutes to play with one of the dogs and use your observations to provide insight into the dogs personality.

A 30-minute rescue takes the shortest amount of time to make a real difference with a shelter dog.

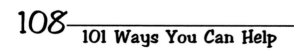

97.

FOR YOUTH & TEENS
Be Prepared For Injuries

At any time, your own dog may be injured. Educate yourself and your family on how to deal with emergency pet injuries. First, purchase a comprehensive, easy-to-read book on animal first-aide. Stay current on basics such as treating bleeding wounds, heat stroke and animal CPR. Make sure everyone in your family knows where the book will be located.

Post the phone numbers of your dogs local vet near your main phone, as well as the phone number and hours of your local "after-hours" animal emergency clinic.

Make a small, yet comprehensive first aide kit for your pet. A basic kit would contain the following:
- tweezers
- scissors
- gloves
- hydrogen peroxide
- antibiotic liquid creme or spray
- nonstick gauze pads and gauze for wrapping
- adhesive tape

98.

Be a Detective

There is one volunteer at the shelter who frequently makes people cry tears of joy. This is the person that searches the huge "lost dog" book checking descriptions to see if any of the reported lost dogs have been checked into the humane society or local shelter. They then call the owners to report the happy news of a "found" dog - to the delight of the distressed owners.

But checking the descriptions of these dogs takes time and dedication. You can volunteer any amount of time to be this "Lost and Found" detective at your local shelter. Call your humane society or shelter to see what qualifications are required for this position.

 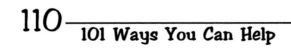

99.

USE YOUR SKILLS
Make Crafts

If you are "crafty," you are in demand. Crafts are always needed as donated items at the shelter. If your humane society has a fund-raising festival, completed craft projects can be used in silent auctions, raffles or in direct to retail sales to the contributors. Contact your local organization and determine their needs and fund-raising calendar to plan your construction calendar.

So, whether you knit, woodwork, sew or paint, you can use your creative passion for your art to benefit your local shelter.

100.

The ULTIMATE Rescue Resource on the Web!

Where can I find the most current breed rescue information, groups and links on the web? There is only one spot that frequently checks links and keeps the pages as up to date as possible and that can be found at:

http://www.ecn.purdue.edu/~laird/animal_rescue/

Kyler Laird started this site around 1990 and it contains resources from breed rescue and shelter groups around the U.S. and worldwide to other resources on starting a shelter and dog rescue newsgroups.

If you need the latest information on these groups, I urge you to visit this site.

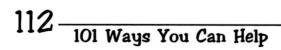

101.

Share Your Love

And last, but by no means least, when you get done reading this page, call your dog and give it a big hug filled with lots of love. If you don't have a dog, call up a rescue group _today_ and volunteer your love and energy.

They give so much to our lives and only desire our attention and kindness. Your love can help them immeasurably and your dedication can change their lives.

So find a dog and give him a scratch behind the ears, spend 5 minutes on a belly rub, throw the frisbee to her – and let them know you love them as much as they love you!

Part 2:

Wish Lists

Wish Lists

OFFICE SUPPLIES

Padded envelopes
Letter Folding machine
Software programs/ clipart
Pre-paid phone cards
Poster paper
Printer/copier paper
Writing pads
Manila folders
Color copier
Calculators
Photo scanner
Walkie-talkies

Camera film
Electric stapler
Digital camera
Laser printer
Envelopes
Pens
Post-It notes
File boxes
Stamps
Instant camera
Portable phone

Office furniture - Chair, desk, cabinets
2-hour uninterruptable power supply
Developing artwork and graphic design for newsletters
Fax machine – all in one – printer/copier/fax
Computer Equipment: Hard drives, ZIP drives disks, and scanner

FACILITIES SUPPLIES

Duct tape
33 gallon wheeled trashcans
Garden hoses-Varying lengths
Clothes washer/dryer
Broom
AM/FM radio
Disinfectant
Night lights and bulbs
Wheel barrow
Little red Wagon
Large laundry baskets
Outdoor thermometer
Construction materials
"Dog-Proof" glass for windows
Electrical help
cages
Paint – all colors

Rubbermaid containers & lids
Dehumidifier
Leaf and rock rakes
Can opener – electric
Dustpan
Air freshener
Wet/Dry Vacuum
Rubber backed bathmat
Weed whacker
Plastic swimming pool
Hand-truck
Patio furniture
Gravel for play yard
Outdoor lighting
Multi-unit stainless steel
Concrete sealant for floors

Potting soil
Trash bags – plastic
Bookcases and shelving
Flooring tile for floors
Toolboxes

Store space for adoptions
Folding table and chairs
Extension cords
Electric can opener
Cameras

New/Used full size pick-up truck or van
Dustbuster
Assorted Tools - wrenches, screwdrivers, drills, socket sets, jigsaw, circular saws, table saws
Perennial plants and half barrels for planter boxes to liven up area

HOUSEHOLD SUPPLIES

Anti-bacterial soap
Laundry detergent
Pine cleaner
Sponges
Paper plates
Pre-paid gas card
Stereo system
Locking file cabinet
Pressure washer
Photo albums
Bleach
Video camera and monitor
Telephone
Window cleaner
"Nature's Miracle"
Stuffed Animals
Old newspaper
Easels

Fabric softener sheets
Dishwashing detergent
Steel wool
Scouring pads
Batteries
Roll away tool box
Blenders
Rain coat
Pots and pans
Warm blankets
Computer and printer
Refrigerator
Paper towels
General purpose cleaner
Aluminum Cans
Furniture
Old silverware

Used children's plastic Jungle gyms
Old blankets, towels, rugs , comforters, flannel sheets

MEDICAL SUPPLIES

Neosporin	Pedialyte
Cotton Balls	Peroxide
Exam gloves	Vitamin C
Vitamin E	Microscope
Q-tips	Medical supplies
Digital thermometer	Stethoscope
Electrolyte	Evaporated milk
Gerber's Rice Baby Cereal	Gauze bandages
Puppy nursing bottles	Updated veterinary texts
Heating pads	Digital baby scale

Small baby bottles and preemie nipples

DOG SUPPLIES

Toys/nylabones/rawhides	Grooming brushes
Nail clippers	Old pillows
Dog crates	Leashes and collars
Pooper Scooper	Shampoo
Washable beds and blankets	Stainless steel bowls
Hair trimmers/blades	Balls
Flexi-leashes	Vari-kennels
Kiddie-pools	Nylabone Chew toys (lg-XL)
Kong or Tuffy toys (lg-XL)	Training treats
Bagged and canned food	Any grooming supplies
Gallons of flea shampoo	

FUNDRAISING IDEAS

Hand-painted silk ties	Greeting cards
Pet beds	Framed dog/cat artwork
Quilt Making	

Used books for book sale fundraisers
Gourmet recipes for dog food/treats

Wish Lists

Part 3:

AKC Breed Groups & Websites

AKC Breed Groups

Rescue Rover!

CS = CORRESPONDING SECR. / RS = RECORDING SECR.

Affenpinscher Club of America
CS : Jo Acton, P.O. Box 31633, Billings, MT , 59107-1633

Afghan Hound Club of America, Inc.
CS : Barbara Bornstein, 6018 E Osborn Rd, Scottsdale, AZ , 85251
Website: trims.com/ahca/

Airedale Terrier Club of America
CS : Linda Baake, 4636 Old Cherry Point Rd, New Bern, NC , 28560
Website: www.Airedale.org

Akita Club of America
CS : Barbara Cicognani, 520 McChesney Ave Ext, Troy, NY , 12180
Website: www.akitaclub.org

Alaskan Malamute Club of America, Inc.
CS: Stephen Piper, 3528 Pinhook Rd, Antioch, TN , 37013-1510
Website: www.members.aol.com/amcahome/amcahome.htm

American Belgian Malinois Club
RS : Stephanie Burns, 1505 G St, Napa, CA , 94559-1142
Website: www.breedclub.org/ABMC.htm

American Belgian Tervuren Club, Inc.
CS : Diane Schultz, RR 1 Box 759, Pomona Park, FL , 32181-9714
Website: www.abtc.org

American Black & Tan Coonhound Club, Inc.
Secr. : Jinnie-Ann Stora, 517 S College Ave, Salina, KS , 67401-4219
Website: www.abtcc.com

American Bloodhound Club
Secr. : Edward Kilby, 1914 Berry Lane, Daytona Beach, FL , 32124
Website: www.bloodhounds.org

American Bouvier des Flandres Club, Inc.
Secretary : David Raper, 1718 Trinity Rd, Raleigh, NC , 27607-4920
Website: www.bouvier.org

American Boxer Club, Inc.
CS: Barbara Wagner, 6310 Edward Dr, Clinton, MD , 20735-4135
Website: clubs.akc.org/abc/abc-home.htm

American Brittany Club, Inc.
CS : Mary Jo Trimble, 10370 Fleming Rd, Carterville, IL , 62918-3350
Website: clubs.akc.org/brit

American Bullmastiff Association, Inc.
CS : Linda Walton, 210 E 12th Ave, Belton, TX , 76513
Website: clubs.akc.org/aba/index.html

American Cavalier King Charles Spaniel Club, Inc.
CS : Martha Guimond, 1905 Upper Ridge Rd, Green Lane, PA , 18054
Website: www.ACKCSC.org

American Chesapeake Club, Inc.
CS: Dyane Baldwin, 4308 Mannsville Road, Newport, PA , 17074
Website: www.amchessieclub.org

American Chinese Crested Club, Inc.
CS : Pat Huhmann, 1277 Chambers Rd, Saint Louis, MO , 63137-1939
Website: amchinesecrestedclub.com

American Eskimo Dog Club of America
CS : Kathleen Bieltz, 1710 Stone Meadows Ln, Houston, TX , 77094
Website: www.members.home.net/jamarsch/aedca

American Fox Terrier Club
CS : Martin Goldstein, P. O. Box 1448, Edison, NJ , 08818-1448
Website: www.aftc.org

American Foxhound Club
Secr. : James Rea, P. O. Box 2588, Clarkesville, GA , 30523-0044
Website: www.crosswinds.net/~foxhound

American Lhasa Apso Club, Inc.
CS : Jan Graunke, 4626 Calumet Ave, Manitowoc, WI , 54220-9358
Website: www.lhasaapso.org

American Maltese Association, Inc.
CS : Barbara Miener, 2523 N Starr St, Tacoma, WA , 98403-2940
Website: www.americanmaltese.org

American Manchester Terrier Club
Secr. : Paula Hradkowsky, 2274 Broomstick Rd, Green Ln, PA , 18054
Website: clubs.akc.org/mtca/index.htm

American Plott Association
Secr. : Brenda Orsbon, 7725 Graysport Crosn, Coffeeville, MS. 3892?

American Pointer Club, Inc.
CS : Karin Ashe, 1914 Parsonage Rd, Parkton, MD , 21120-9679
Website: www.americanpointerclub.org

American Polish Lowland Sheepdog
CS : Phyllis Vlasaty, 7586 SW 93rd St Rd , Ocala, FL , 34476
Website: www.aponc.com

American Pomeranian Club, Inc.
CS : Cynthia Boulware, 6450 Rolling Heights Cir, Kaufman, TX , 75142
Website: www.geocities.com/Petsburgh/Haven/3419/index.html

American Rottweiler Club
Secr.: Pamela Grant, 45 Erica Ln, Belen, NM , 87002-2829
Website: www.amrottclub.org

American Sealyham Terrier Club
CS : Sandra Kroll, 920 Pleasant Ave, Highland Park, IL , 60035-4616
Website: clubs.akc.org/sealy

American Shetland Sheepdog Association
CS : Beverly Muhlenhaupt, 7274 S Chase Way, Littleton, CO , 80128
Website: www.assa.org

American Shih Tzu Club, Inc.
CS : Bonnie Prato, 5252 Shafter Ave, Oakland, CA , 94618-1051
Website: clubs.akc.org/astc/index.html

American Spaniel Club, Inc.
CS : Ann Martin, 287 Castle Terrace, Lyndhurst, NJ , 07071-2001
Website: www.asc-cockerspaniel.org

American Toy Fox Terrier Club
CS : Margi Hill, 270 Edward Dr, Bellefonte, PA , 16823-8581

American Water Spaniel Club
CS : Linda Hattrem, 5799 40th St, Princeton, MN , 55371-6440
Website: www.starsouth.com/awsc

American Whippet Club, Inc.
Secr. : Lori Nelson, 31838 N 52nd St., Cave Creek, AZ , 85331
Website: breedclub.org/AWC.htm

American Wirehaired Pointing Griffon Association
CS : Patricia Loomis, 7920 Peters Rd, Jacksonville, AR , 72076-2166
Website: www.awpga.com

Anatolian Shepherd Dog Club of America
CS : Quinn Harned, 845 Chariot Trail, Limestone, TN , 37681
Website: www.asdca.org

Australian Cattle Dog Club of America
CS : Pamela Mansfield, 5041 Britton Ln, Jacksonville, FL , 32210
Website: www.acdca.org

Australian Terrier Club of America, Inc.
CS : Kim Occhiuti, 5 Noonhill Rd, Medfield, MA , 02052-3007
Website: www.australianterrier.org

Basenji Club of America, Inc.
CS : Anne Graves, 5102 Darnell St, Houston, TX , 77096-1404
Website: www.basenji.org

Basset Hound Club of America, Inc.
CS : Carol Makowski, 9007 Tahoe Ln, Boulder, CO , 80301-5146
Website: www.basset-bhca.org

Bearded Collie Club of America, Inc.
CS : Lynn Zagarella, 1620 Stagecoach Cir, Elizabeth, CO , 80107
Website: www.beardie.net/bcca

Bedlington Terrier Club of America
CS : Lucy Heyman, 19402 Kuykendahl Rd, Spring, TX , 77379-3406
Website: clubs.akc.org/btca

Belgian Sheepdog Club of America, Inc.
CS : Carol Morris, 8315 Cave City Rd., Mountain Ranch, CA , 95246
Website: www.mint.net/~dspang/bsca.html

Bernese Mountain Dog Club of America, Inc.
Secr. : Mary Durham, P.O. Box 1158, Groton, MA , 01450
Website: www.bmd.org/bmdca.html

Bichon Frise Club of America, Inc.
CS : Joanne Styles, 32 Oak St, Centereach, NY , 11720
Website: www.bichon.org

Border Collie Society of America
Secr : Sharon Ferguson, 9002 Sovereign Rd, San Diego, CA ,92123
Website: www.bordercolliesociety.com

Border Terrier Club of America, Inc.
CS :Joann Frier-Murza, 131 Bordentown Rd, Crosswicks, NJ, 08515
Website: clubs.akc.org/btcoa

Borzoi Club of America, Inc.
CS : Karen Mays, 29 Crown Dr, Warren, NJ , 07059-5111
Website: www.borzoiclubofamerica.com

Boston Terrier Club of America, Inc.
CS : Frederick Comstock, 36 Twin Lakes Dr, Waterford, CT , 06385
Website: www.bostonterrierclubofamerica.org/index.htm

Briard Club of America, Inc.
Secr. : M Lana Sheer, P O Box 1123, Chadds Ford, PA , 19317
Website: clubs.akc.org/bca

Bull Terrier Club of America
CS : Rebecca Poole, 2630 Gold Point Cir, Hixson, TN , 37343-1831
Website: www.btca.com

Bulldog Club of America
CS : Ray Knudson, 4300 Town Rd, Salem, WI , 53168-9233
Website: www.thebca.org

Cairn Terrier Club of America
CS : Christine Bowlus, 6152 Golf Club Rd, Howell, MI , 48843-9012
Website: www.cairnterrier.org

Canaan Dog Club of America
CS: Sally Armstrong-Barnhardt, 2300 Crosovr Rd, Reno, NV , 89510
Website: www.cdca.org

Cardigan Welsh Corgi Club of America, Inc.
CS : Cathryn Ochs-Cline, 11306 Geddys Ct, Reston, VA , 20191-3606
Website: www.cardigancorgis.com

Chihuahua Club of America, Inc.
CS : Diana Garren, 16 Hillgirt Rd, Hendersonville, NC , 28792-1171
Website: www.chihuahuaclubofamerica.com

Chinese Shar-Pei Club of America, Inc.
CS : Susan Lauder, 1249 Old Dairy Rd, Summerville, SC , 29483-7419
Website: www.cspca.com

Chow Chow Club, Inc.
CS: Cindy Conover, 48 Miller Street, Phillipsburg, NJ , 08865
Website: www.chowclub.org

Clumber Spaniel Club of America, Inc.
Secr. : Kimberly Jordan, 2901 Shady Ave, Pittsburgh, PA , 15217
Website: www.clumbers.org

Collie Club of America, Inc.
Secr. : Carmen Leonard, 1119 S Fleming Rd., Woodstock, IL , 60098
Website: www.collieclubofamerica.org

Curly-Coated Retriever Club of America
CS: Marilyn Smith, 251 NW 151st Ave, Pmbk Pines, FL , 33028-1809
Website: www.ccrca.org

Dachshund Club of America, Inc.
Secr.: Andra O'Connell, 1793 Berme Road, Kerhonkson, NY , 12446
Website: www.dachshund-dca.org

Dalmatian Club of America, Inc.
CS: Sharon Boyd, 2316 Mccrary Rd, Richmond, TX , 77469-9696
Website: www.thedca.org

Dandie Dinmont Terrier Club of America, Inc.
CS: Gail Isner, 151 Junaluska Dr, Woodstock, GA , 30188-3135
Website: clubs.akc.org/ddtca/index.html

Doberman Pinscher Club of America
CS: John Schoeneman, 4309 Caldwell Ln, Charlotte, NC , 28269
Website: www.dpca.org

English Cocker Spaniel Club of America, Inc.
CS: Kate Romanski, P. O. Box 252, Hales Corners, WI , 53130-0252
Website: www.ecsca.org

English Foxhound Club of America
CS: John Wickline, 13311 Williams Dr, Brandywine, MD , 20613-7861

English Setter Association of America, Inc.
CS: Dawn Ronyak, 114 Burlington Oval Dr, Chardon, OH , 44024
Website: www.esaa.com

English Springer Spaniel Field Trial Association, Inc.
Secr.: Barbara Boettcher, P O Box 1590, Milton , WA , 98354-1802
Website: www.essfta.org

English Toy Spaniel Club of America
CS: Karen Pouder, 19121 12th Ave N, East Moline, IL , 61244
Website: www.kenjockety.com/etsca

Field Spaniel Society of America
CS : Suzanne Fernau, 549 Main Rd, Johns Island, SC , 29455-3412
Website: clubs.akc.org/fssa/index/html

Rescue Rover!

Finnish Spitz Club of America
Secr.: Leslie Carlson, 23 Grand Canyon Dr., Los Alamos, NM , 87544
Website: www.99main.com/~storzw

Flat-Coated Retriever Society of America, Inc.
CS : Joan Dever, 13208 Mandarin Rd, Jacksonville, FL , 32223-1746
Website: www.fcrsainc.org

French Bulldog Club of America
CS : Vicki Kerr, 860 N 100th W, Valpariso, IN , 46395
Website: www.frenchbulldogclub.org

German Pinscher Club of America
CS : Marilyn Marchwicki, 6657 Flat River Rd, Greene, RI , 02827-2012

German Shepherd Dog Club of America
CS : Blanche Beisswenger, 17 W Ivy Ln, Englewood, NJ , 07631-1721
Website: www.gsdca.org

German Shorthaired Pointer Club of America
CS : Susan Clemons, P. O. Box 3958, Chino Valley, AZ , 86323-2721
Website: www.gspca.org

German Wirehaired Pointer Club of America, Inc.
CS : Barbara Tucker, P. O. Box 677, Grass Lake, MI , 49240-0677
Website: www.gwpca.com

Giant Schnauzer Club of America, Inc.
CS : Barbara Moeller, 36 Staples Shore Rd, Lakeville, MA , 02347-1647
Website: clubs.akc.org/gsca/

Golden Retriever Club of America
CS: Dianne Barnes. P. O. Box 932, Bonner, MT , 59823-0932
Website: www.grca.org

Gordon Setter Club of America, Inc.
CS: Carolyn Gold, 2001 Nicasio Valley Rd, Nicasio, CA , 94946-9725
Website: www.gsca.org

Great Dane Club of America, Inc.
CS : Sue Mahany, 11407 N State Route 91, Dunlap, IL , 61525-9727
Website: www.gdca.org

Great Pyrenees Club of America, Inc.
Secr. : Janet Ingram, 204 Wild Partridge Ln, Radford, VA , 24141
Website: www.akc.org/gpca

Greater Swiss Mountain Dog Club of America, Inc.
CS : Karen Becker, 11670 Milwaukee St, Denver, CO , 80233-2444
Website: www.gsmdca.org

Greyhound Club of America
CS : Beth Gordon, P. O. Box 850, La Luz, NM , 88337-0850
Website: www.greyhoundclubofamerica.org

Havanese Club of America
CS : Dee Dee Petty, 30140 Antelope Rd. # D 439, Menitee, CA , 92584
Website: www.havanese.org

Ibizan Hound Club of the United States
CS : Stephanie Bonner, 3098 Elm Rd, Duluth, MN , 55804-3065
Website: www.geocities.com/Heartland/Pointe/2446/IHCUS.htm

Irish Setter Club of America, Inc.
CS : Jeanette Holmes, 5389 Harrison Rd, Paradise, CA , 95969-6612
Website: www.irishsetterclub.org

Irish Terrier Club of America
CS : Cory Rivera, : 22720 Perry St, Perris, CA , 92570-8925
Website: www.dogbiz.com/itca/

Irish Water Spaniel Club of America
Secr. : Rosemary Sexton, 209 Morton Avenue, Elk River, MN , 55330
Website: clubs.akc.org/iwsc/

Irish Wolfhound Club of America
CS : Shirley Pfarrer, 8855 US Rt 40, New Carlisle, OH , 45344-9682
Website: www.iwclubofamerica.org

Italian Greyhound Club of America, Inc.
CS : Lilian Barber, 35648 Menifee Rd, Murrieta, CA , 92563-2356
Website: www.italiangreyhound.org

Jack Russell Terrier Association of America
CS : Sandy Peterson, RR 2 Box 202, Williamsport, PA , 17701
Website: www.jrtaa.org

Japanese Chin Club of America
CS : Maxine Yager, 10021 SE Shadden Rd, Overbrook, KS , 66524
Website: www.japanesechin.org

Keeshond Club of America, Inc.
CS : Bonnie Bell, 2872 A West Long Dr, Littleton, CO , 80120
Website: www.keeshond.org

Rescue Rover!

Komondor Club of America, Inc.
CS : Linda Patrick, 4695 Peckins Rd, Chelsea, MI , 48118-9200
Website: clubs.akc.org/kca/

Kuvasz Club of America
CS : Susan Gilmore, P. O. Box 90, Braceville, IL , 60407-0090
Website: www.kuvasz.com

Labrador Retriever Club, Inc.
Secr:Christopher Wincek,25555 Som CtrRd,Hunting Valley,OH, 44022
Website: www.thelabradorclub.com

Lowchen Club of America
CS : Jo Allyn Beckett, 17381 Banyon Ln, Lake Oswego, OR , 97034

Mastiff Club of America, Inc.
CS : Sherry White, P. O. Box 14067, Colorado Springs, CO , 80914
Website: www.mastiff.org

Miniature Bull Terrier Club of America
CS : Pat Chesser, 545 Canyon Rd, Wetumpka, AL , 36093-1406

Miniature Pinscher Club of America, Inc.
CS : Bonnie Goetz, W7201 Cty Trunk E, Beaver Dam, WI , 53916-0000
Website: www.minpin.org

National Beagle Club
CS : Susan Stone, P. O. Box 13, Middleburg, VA , 20118-0013
Website: clubs.akc.org/NBC/index.htm

National Shiba Club of America
CS : Karen Drentlaw, 1723 Mills St, Black Earth, WI , 53515-9425
Website: www.shibas.org/index.html

Newfoundland Club of America, Inc.
CS : Robin Seaman, 107 New St, Rehoboth, MA , 02769-2900
Website: www.geocities.com/newfdogclub/w_main_jump.htm

Norwegian Elkhound Association of America, Inc.
CS : Leslie Forrest, 21738 N Hampton Ct, Kildeer, IL , 60047
Website: www.neaa.com

Norwich and Norfolk Terrier Club
CS : Jean Kessler, 12620 Garman Dr, Nokesville, VA , 20181

Old English Sheepdog Club of America, Inc.
CS : Holly McIntire, 9906 E Arizona Dr #1015, Denver, CO , 80231
Website: clubs.akc.org/oesca

Otterhound Club of America
CS : Dian Quist-Sulek, Rt 1, Box 247, Palmyra, NE , 68418
Website: clubs.akc.org/ohca/

Papillon Club of America, Inc.
CS : June Peterson, 7232 East Richter Lane, New Ulm, TX , 78950
Website: www.papillonclub.org

Pekingese Club of America, Inc.
Secr:Leonie Schultz, 19726 Rainbow Ridge Rd, Bergton, VA , 22811
Website: www.geocities.com/Heartland/3843

Pembroke Welsh Corgi Club of America, Inc.
CS: Joan Reid, 9589 Sheldon Road, Elk Grove, CA , 95624-1442
Website: www.pembrokecorgi.org

Petit Basset Griffon Vendeen Club of America
Secr. : Dorothy Allen, 25 Beth Dr, Moorestown, NJ , 08057-3021
Website: www.pbgv.org

Pharaoh Hound Club of America
CS: Rita Sacks, P. O. Box 895454, Leesburg, FL , 34789-5454

Poodle Club of America, Inc.
CS: Thomas Carneal, 418 W 2nd St, Maryville, MO , 64468-2233
Website: www.swdg.com/pca

Portuguese Water Dog Club of America, Inc.
CS: Clair De Christina, 1745 Tower Dr, Stoughton, WI , 53589-3537
Website: www.pwdca.org

Pug Dog Club of America, Inc.
Secr. : Janet McLaughlin, 176 Sunset Dr, Glastonbury, CT , 06033
Website: www.pugs.org

Puli Club of America, Inc.
CS: Sandra Schickedanz, P. O. Box 2806, Edmond, OK , 73083-2806

Rhodesian Ridgeback Club of the United States, Inc.
CS : Bonnie Louden, P. O. Box 37, Columbia, MD , 21045
Website: rrcus.org

Saluki Club of America
Secr. : Diana Farmer, 9787 N 52nd St, Riley, KS , 66531-9604
Website: www.saluki.org

Samoyed Club of America, Inc.
CS : Sheila Herrmann, 85222 Highway 437, Covington, LA , 70435
Website: www.samoyed.org/Samoyed_Club_of_America.html

Schipperke Club of America, Inc.
CS : Catherine Ryan, 10 Pomper Dr, E Northport, NY , 11731-6420
Website: clubs.akc.org/schip

Scottish Deerhound Club of America, Inc.
Secr. : Debra Narwold, P. O. Box 272, Kelley, IA , 50134-0272
Website: www.deerhound.org

Scottish Terrier Club of America
CS : Lois Bolding, 1212 Lake Charles Cir, Lutz, FL , 33549-4717
Website: clubs.akc.org/stca

Siberian Husky Club of America, Inc.
CS : Fain Zimmerman, 210 Madera St, Victoria, TX , 77905-0611
Website: www.shca.org

Silky Terrier Club of America, Inc.
CS : Louise Rosewell, 2783 S Saulsbury St, Denver, CO , 80227
Website: www.geocities.com/silkyterrierclubofamerica/index.html

Skye Terrier Club of America
Secr. : Karen J'Anthony, P. O. Box 295, Camden, DE , 19934-0295
Website: clubs.akc.org/skye

Soft Coated Wheaten Terrier Club of America
CS: Gene Kline, 585 Timberlane Rd, Wetumpka, AL , 36093-1663
Website: www.scwtca.org

Spinone Club of America
CS : Bridget Curry, 1505 Cypress Ln, Davis, CA , 95616-1317
Website: www.spinone.com

St. Bernard Club of America, Inc.
CS : Marilyn Santell, 735 Gp Easterly NE, Cortland, OH , 44410-0000
Website: clubs.akc.org/saints/

Staffordshire Bull Terrier Club, Inc.
Secr. : Dianna Caulk, 344 Ramah Rd, Bridgeton, NJ , 08302-6948
Website: clubs.akc.org/sbtci

Staffordshire Terrier Club of America
Corresponding SecretarySCO , 80615-0000
Website: www.amstaff.org

Standard Schnauzer Club of America
Secr. : Annamarie Appel, 9 Woodland Dr., Port Jervis, NY , 12771
Website: www.geocities.com/Yosemite/7068

Sussex Spaniel Club of America
CS : Sylvia Schlueter, 383 Blane Ct, Dawson, IL , 62520-3379

Tibetan Spaniel Club of America
CS : Cheryl Kelly, 3039 Hance Rd, Macedon, NY , 14502-9379
Website: www.tibbies.net/tsca

Tibetan Terrier Club of America, Inc.
Secr. : Peggy Kunau, 55 Stevens Hill Rd, Nottingham, NH , 03290
Website: clubs.akc.org/ttca

United States Australian Shepherd Association
Secr. : Leon Goetz, 2100 Stemmons Fwy Ste 2111, Dallas, TX , 75207
Website: www.australianshepherds.org

United States Kerry Blue Terrier Club, Inc.
CS : Gene Possidento, 1 Park Ln, West Nyack, NY , 10994-2707
Website: kbt.ralden.com/USKBTC/USKBTC.html

United States Lakeland Terrier Club
CS : Edna Lawicki, 8207 E Cholla St, Scottsdale, AZ , 85260
Website: clubs.akc.org/usltc/index.htm

Vizsla Club of America, Inc.
CS : Kim Himmelfarb, 16 Deer Run Road, Collinsville, CT , 06022
Website: clubs.akc.org/vizsla

Weimaraner Club of America
CS : Dorothy Derr Sec, P. O. Box 2907, Muskogee, OK , 74402-2907
Website: www.geocities.com/~weimclub

Welsh Springer Spaniel Club of America, Inc.
CS : Karen Lyle. W254N4989 Mckerrow Dr, Pewaukee, WI, 53072
Website: clubs.akc.org/wssca

Welsh Terrier Club of America, Inc.
CS : Becky Eterno, 14105 N. 87th St., Longmont, CO , 80503-8843
Website: clubs.akc.org/wtca

West Highland White Terrier Club of America
RS : Daphne Gentry, 1826 Manakin Rd, Manakin Sabot, VA , 23103
Website: www.westieclubamerica.com

Yorkshire Terrier Club of America, Inc.
CS : Shirley Patterson, 2 Chestnut Ct., Pottstown, PA , 19465
Website: www.ytca.org

Part 4:

Regional Rescue Groups

Regional Rescue Groups

TO HAVE YOUR BREED PLACEMENT OR RESCUE GROUP LISTED HERE OR TO MAKE CHANGES TO EXISTING LISTINGS, PLEASE FILL OUT THE CHANGE/ ADDITION FORMS PROVIDED IN SECTION 5.

ALASKA

Alaska Humane Society, 5211 Mockingbird Drive, # 210, Anchorage, AK 99507, (907) 344-8808

Friends of Pets, 4711 South Bragaw Street, Anchorage, AK 99507, (907) 562-2535

Gastineau Humane Society, 7705 Glacier Highway, Juneau, AK 99801, (907) 789-0260

Pet Pride, 1598 Wolverine Lane, Fairbanks, AK 99709, (907) 457-7198

SPCA, 7309 Arctic Boulevard, Anchorage, AK 99518, (907) 344-3622

ALABAMA

Alabama Animal Adoption Society, 2808 Crescent Avenue, Homewood, AL 35209, (205) 871-6351

Ark Inc, 3609 Memorial Parkway Southwest, Huntsville, AL 35801, (256) 882-6609

Bessemer Humane Society, 1230 15th Avenue North, Bessemer, AL 35020, (205) 425-0610

Birmingham Humane Society, 1713 Lomb Avenue, Birmingham, AL 35208, (205) 780-7281

Bullock Company Humane Society, Highway 29 South, Union Springs, AL 36089, (334) 738-2432

Chilton County Humane Society, 139 Shade Tree Drive, Clanton, AL 35045, (205) 755-9170

Cullman County Humane Society, 935 Convent Road Northeast, Cullman, AL 35055, (256) 734-9418

Humane Society, 3265 Fairfax Bypass Road, Valley, AL 36854, (334) 756-9377

Humane Society of Elmore County, 255 Central Plank Road, Wetumpka, AL 36092, (334) 567-3377

Humane Society-Greater Huntsville, 2812 Johnson Road SW # A, Huntsville, AL 35805, (256) 881-8081

Humane Society-Etowah County, 1700 Chestnut Street, Gadsden, AL 35901, (256) 547-4846

Lake Martin Humane Society, 2502 Sugarcreek Road, Alexander City, AL 35010, (256) 234-5533

Monroe County Animal Shelter, 2265 Highway 47, Monroeville, AL 36460, (334) 575-3427

Montgomery County Humane Soc., 1150 John Overton Dr, Montgomery, AL 36110, (334) 409-0622

Shelby County Mobile Adoptions, 2652 Valleydale Road, Birmingham, AL 35244, (205) 408-0250

SPCA, 307 Glenwood Street, Mobile, AL 36606, (334) 476-7722

Tailwagger Adoption Center, 7580 Crestwood Boulevard, Birmingham, AL 35210, (205) 595-7281

Walker County Humane Society, 2302 Birmingham Avenue, Jasper, AL 35501, (205) 221-6621

Wiregrass Humane Society, PO Box 1045, Dothan, AL 36302, (334) 792-6693

ARKANSAS

Garland County Animal Welfare, 1249 Ault Loop, Lonsdale, AR 72087, (501) 623-5012

Good Shepherd Humane Society, 40 Armstrong Street, Eureka Springs, AR 72632, (501) 253-9115

Heber Springs Humane Society, 49 Shelter Lane, Heber Springs, AR 72543, (501) 362-7322

Humane Society of Searcy, 112 West Johnston Road, Searcy, AR 72143, (501) 268-3535

Humane Society, 7600 Bauxite Highway, Bauxite, AR 72011, (501) 557-5518

Humane Society, 101 East Semmes Avenue, Osceola, AR 72370, (870) 563-9816

Humane Society, 407 East Nursery Road, Rogers, AR 72758, (501) 636-3703

Humane Society of The Ozark, 103 North College Avenue, Fayetteville, AR 72701, (501) 444-7387

Humane Society of Clark Company, Clark County Road 76, Arkadelphia, AR 71923, (870) 245-2579

Humane Society of Pulaski County, 14600 Colonel Glenn Road, Little Rock, AR 72210, (501) 227-6166

Humane Society, 2656 Highway 201 North, Mountain Home, AR 72653, (870) 425-4660

Humane Society-NE AR, 807 Strawfloor Drive, Jonesboro, AR 72401, (870) 932-5185

Ozark Humane Society, 118 Ridge Avenue, Harrison, AR 72601, (870) 741-8752

Polk County Humane Society, Old Line Road, Mena, AR 71953, (501) 394-5682

Sebastian City Humane Society, 3800 Kelley Highway, Fort Smith, AR 72904, (501) 783-4395

ARIZONA

Animal League of Green Valley, 101 S. LA Canada Dr # 49B, Green Valley, AZ 85614, (520) 625-3170

Animals Benefit Club of AZ, 3111 East Saint John Road, Phoenix, AZ 85032, (602) 867-2169

Arizona Animal Welfare League, 30 North 40th Place, Phoenix, AZ 85034, (602) 273-6850

Arizona Humane Society, 9226 North 13th Avenue, Phoenix, AZ 85021, (602) 997-7585

Arizona Petline, 8026 North 19th Avenue, Phoenix, AZ 85021, (602) 252-2727

Arizona Society For-Prevention, PO Box 33334, Phoenix, AZ 85067, (602) 246-8280

Critter Crater Rescue Ranch, 4 South Beaver Street # 2, Flagstaff, AZ 86001, (520) 913-0582

Doing Things For Animals Inc, PO Box 2165, Sun City, AZ 85372, (623) 977-5793

Humane Society of Sedona Inc, 2115 Shelby Drive, Sedona, AZ 86336, (520) 282-4679

Humane Society of Tucson, 3450 North Kelvin Boulevard, Tucson, AZ 85716, (520) 327-6088

Humane Society-Coconino Association, 3501 East Butler Avenue, Flagstaff, AZ 86004, (520) 526-1076

Lake Havasu City Animal Control, 1100 Empire Drive, Lake Havasu City, AZ 86404, (520) 855-7479

Mohave Company Animal Control, 9880 Vanderslice, Mohave Valley, AZ 86440, (520) 768-3125

Mohave County Animal Control, 950 Buchanan Street, Kingman, AZ 86401, (520) 753-2770

Payson Humane Society Inc, 812 South McLane Road, Payson, AZ 85541, (520) 474-5590

Pet Pride of AZ , 1225 East Broadway Road, Tempe, AZ 85282, (602) 631-5600

Santa Cruz Humane Society, 232 Patatonia Highway, Nogales, AZ 85621, (520) 287-9794

SPCA of Arizona Inc, 220 East Duval Road, Green Valley, AZ 85614, (520) 625-1560

St Johns Animal Control, 703 West 4th North, St Johns, AZ 85936, (520) 337-3165

Valley Humane Society, 15699 West Aniceto Road, Casa Grande, AZ 85222, (520) 836-0904

Verde Valley Humane Society, 1502 West Mingus Avenue, Cottonwood, AZ 86326, (520) 634-7387

Western Arizona Humane Society, 1100 Empire Drive, Lake Havasu City, AZ 86404, (520) 855-5083

Yavapai Humane Society, 1625 Sundog Ranch Road, Prescott, AZ 86301, (520) 445-2666

Yuma County Humane Society, 285 North Figueroa Avenue, Yuma, AZ 85364, (520) 782-1621

CALIFORNIA

A-Pal Humane Society, PO Box 190, Jackson, CA 95642, (209) 223-0410

Adopt-A-Friend, PO Box 1355, Lafayette, CA 94549, (925) 284-8449

AKI Foundation, PO Box 620208, Woodside, CA 94062, (650) 851-0408

Animal Ark of California Soc, 45455 Rosamond Hills, Anza, CA 92539, (909) 763-5900

Animal Emergency Facility, 1736 South Sepulveda Blvd, # A, Los Angeles, CA 90025, (310) 473-1561

Animal Outreach Of Mother Lode, 6200 Enterprise Dr # D, Diamond Springs, CA 95619, (530) 642-2287

Animal Place, 3448 Laguna Creek Trail, Vacaville, CA 95688, (707) 449-4814

Animal Rescue Foundation, 2780 Mitchell Drive, Walnut Creek, CA 94598 , (925) 256-1273

Animal Services Auxiliary, 2846 Finch Road, Modesto, CA 95354, (209) 524-0669

Animal Shelter SPCA, 103 South Hughes Avenue, Fresno, CA 93706, (559) 233-7722

Animal Welfare Information, Panetta Road & Meadow Place, Carmel Valley, CA 93924, (831) 659-3238

Animal Welfare Association, PO Box 410120, San Francisco, CA 94141, (415) 771-1649

Animals At Risk Care Sanctuary, PO Box 578763, Modesto, CA 95357, (209) 527-2272

Ark Trust Inc, 5551 Balboa Boulevard, Encino, CA 91316, (818) 501-2275

ASPCA, 1111 North Brand Boulevard, Glendale, CA 91202 , (818) 241-7853

Barstow Humane Society, 31339 Main Street, Barstow, CA 92311, (760) 252-4800

Berkeley-East Bay Humane Soc , 2700 9th Street, Berkeley, CA 94710, (510) 845-7735

Big Bear Valley Humane Society , PO Box 1724, Big Bear Lake, CA 92315 , (909) 866-5555

CARE - Companion Animal Rescue Effort, P.O. Box 111474 Campbell, CA 95011-1474

Central Coast Animal Society , 150 South 13th Street # D, Grover Beach, CA 93433 , (805) 481-1433

Coalition To Protect Animals, PO Box 2448, Riverside, CA 92516 , (909) 682-7872

Companion Pet Retreat , 22902 Los Alisos Boulevard, Mission Viejo, CA 92691, (949) 707-1204

Concerned Animal Lovers Association , 2500 Fender Avenue # I, Fullerton, CA 92831, (714) 738-4832

Contra Costa Humane Society, 1008 Oak Hill Road, Lafayette, CA 94549, (925) 284-8586

Crestline Critter Humane Soc , 23987 Lake Drive, Crestline, CA 92325, (909) 338-3410

D.E.L.T.A., P.O. Box 9, Glendale, CA 91209, (818) 241-6282

El Dorado Humane Society, 484 Pleasant Valley Road, Diamond Springs, CA 95619, (530) 642-2738

Friends For Pets Foundation, 11117 Fleetwood Street, Sun Valley, CA 91352, (818) 767-5919

Friends of Animals Foundation, 2336 South Sepulveda Blvd, Los Angeles, CA 90064, (310) 479-5089

Friends-Fairmont Animal Shltr, 2700 Fairmont Drive, San Leandro, CA 94578, (510) 352-0598

Friendship Foundation, PO Box 6525, Albany, CA 94706, (510) 528-9104

Glendale Humane Society, 717 Ivy Street, Glendale, CA 91204, (818) 242-1128

Haven Humane Society, 7449 Eastside Road, Redding, CA 96001, (530) 241-1653

Hayward Animal Control Office, 16 Barnes Court, Hayward, CA 94544, (510) 293-7200

Hayward Friends of Animals, PO Box 3986, Hayward, CA 94540 , (510) 886-7546

Homeless Animal Rescue Team, PO Box 1394, Cambria, CA 93428, (805) 927-1358

Humane Education Network , PO Box 7434, Menlo Park, CA 94026, (650) 854-8921

Humane Society , 4590 South Highway 99, Stockton, CA 95215, (209) 466-0339

Humane Society, 763 West Highland Avenue, San Bernardino, CA 92405, (909) 882-2934

Humane Society, 1121 Sonoma Boulevard, Vallejo, CA 94590, (707) 645-7905

Humane Society of San Bernardino, 763 W. Highland Ave, San Bernardino, CA 92405, (909) 886-5026

Humane Society of Santa Clara, 2530 Lafayette Street, Santa Clara, CA 95050, (408) 727-3383

Humane Society Golden Empire, PO Box 817, Grass Valley, CA 95945, (530) 273-9489

Humane Society of Del Norte, 1900 West Washington Blvd, Crescent City, CA 95531, (707) 464-1686

Humane Society Town & Country, County Road 99, Orland, CA 95963, (530) 865-3661

Humane Society of Truckee, PO Box 9041, Truckee, CA 96162, (530) 587-5948

Humane Society Thrift Shop, 240 East Highland Avenue, San Bernardino, CA 92404, (909) 881-2532

Humane Society of The Redwoods, 909 Redwood Drive, Garberville, CA 95542, (707) 923-0167

Humane Society-Sonoma County, 5345 Sebastopol Road, Santa Rosa, CA 95407, (707) 542-0882

Humane Society-Calaveras, PO Box 216, Hathaway Pines, CA 95233, (209) 795-3659

Humane Society-Imperial Valley, 1575 West Pico Avenue, El Centro, CA 92243, (760) 352-1911

Humane Society-Ventura County, 402 Bryant Street, Ojai, CA 93023, (805) 646-6505

IWV Humane Society, 411 San Bernardino Boulevard, Ridgecrest, CA 93555, (760) 375-9302

Lake Elsinore Animal Control, 29001 Bastron Avenue, Lake Elsinore, CA 92530, (909) 674-0618

Lake Isabella Animal Shelter, 4621 Lake Isabella Boulevard, Lake Isabella, CA 93240, (760) 379-1696

Lulu Belle Animal Haven, 2549 Dogwood Road, El Centro, CA 92243, (760) 355-4125

Mercy Crusade Inc , PO Box 4374, Thousand Oaks, CA 91359, (818) 597-2926

Mountains Humane Society, PO Box 452, Lake Arrowhead, CA 92352, (909) 337-6422

National Animal Protection, PO Box 271, Napa, CA 94559, (707) 252-0362

New Hope For Animals, 9123 Hazen Drive, Beverly Hills, CA 90210, (310) 271-6092

Nike Animal Rescue Foundation, P.O. Box 26587, San Jose, CA 95159, 408.224.6273

North County Humane Society, 2300 Ramona Road, Atascadero, CA 93422, (805) 466-5403

Oakland Society-Cruelty Anmls, 8323 Baldwin Street, Oakland, CA 94621, (510) 569-0702

Ohlone Humane Society, 39120 Argonaut Way # 108, Fremont, CA 94538, (510) 490-4587

Orange County Humane Society, 21632 Newland Street, Huntington Beach, CA 92646, (714) 536-8480

Pal-Animal Sanctuary, 11959 Mariposa Road # 4, Hesperia, CA 92345, (760) 948-1125

Palo Alto Humane Society, 415 Cambridge Avenue, Palo Alto, CA 94306, (650) 327-0631

Pasadena Humane Society, 361 South Raymond Avenue, Pasadena, CA 91105, (626) 792-7151

Peninsula Humane Society, 12 Airport Boulevard, San Mateo, CA 94401, (650) 340-8200

Pet Adoption Fund, 7507 Deering Avenue, Canoga Park, CA 91303, (818) 340-1687

Pet Adoption League, PO Box 3303, Grass Valley, CA 95945, (530) 273-7958

Pet Assistance Foundation, PO Box 264, La Mesa, CA 91944, (619) 697-7387

Pet Lifeline, 749 Sutter Street, Yuba City, CA 95991, (530) 755-1437

Pet Rescue Association, 8906 Norris Avenue, Sun Valley, CA 91352 , (818) 845-6222

Pets In Need, 873 5th Avenue, Redwood City, CA 94063, (650) 367-1405

Pets N Friends, 10182 I Avenue # D, Hesperia, CA 92345, (760) 244-4430

Piedra Foundation, 4211 Holly Lane, Bonsall, CA 92003, (760) 726-9206

Pomona Valley Humane Society, West Mission Blvd & Humane Way, Pomona, CA 91766, (909) 623-9777

Ramona Animal Shelter Inc, 690 Humane Way, San Jacinto, CA 92582, (909) 925-1204

Rancho Coastal Humane Society, 389 Requeza Street, Encinitas, CA 92024, (760) 753-6413

Redlands Humane Society Inc , PO Box 1212, Redlands, CA 92373, (909) 792-6199

Rohnert Park Animal Shelter, 301 J Rogers Lane, Rohnert Park, CA 94928, (707) 584-1582

San Diego Humane Society, 887 Sherman Street, San Diego, CA 92110, (619) 299-7012

San Francisco SPCA, 2500-16th Street, San Francisco, CA 94103, (415) 554-3000

Santa Barbara Humane Society, 5399 Overpass Road, Santa Barbara, CA 93111, (805) 964-4777

Santa Cruz Humane Society, 2200 7th Avenue, Santa Cruz, CA 95062, (831) 475-6454

Santa Maria Valley Humane Society, 751 Black Road, Santa Maria, CA 93458, (805) 349-3435

Santa Ynez Valley Humane Society, 111 Commerce Drive, Buellton, CA 93427, (805) 688-8224

Sequoia Humane Society, 6073 Loma Avenue, Eureka, CA 95503, (707) 442-1782

Society-Prevention of Cruelty , 2500 16th Street, San Francisco, CA 94103, (415) 554-3000

Solano County Friends-Animals, PO Box 4081, Vallejo, CA 94590 , (707) 552-3323

South Bay IN Defense-Animals, PO Box 41443, San Jose, CA 95160, (408) 927-9281

South Lake Tahoe Humane Soc ,1063 Magua Street, South Lake Tahoe, CA 96150, (530) 577-4521

Spay Neuter Assistance Program, PO Box 1355, Lafayette, CA 94549, (925) 284-8141

SPCA , 3000 Gibson Street ,Bakersfield, CA 93308, (661) 324-3209

SPCA Haven-Of Solano County, 2200 Peabody Road, Vacaville, CA 95687 ,(707) 448-7722

SPCA Humane Society, 1002 Monterey Salinas Highway, Monterey, CA 93940, (831) 373-2631

SPCA LA, 5026 West Jefferson Boulevard, Los Angeles, CA 90016, (323) 730-5300

SPCA of Mariposa County, 5599 State Highway 49 North, Mariposa, CA 95338, (209) 966-5275

SPCA of Stanislaus, 4733 Yosemite Boulevard, Modesto, CA 95357, (209) 575-2918

SPCA Sacramento Society, 6201 Florin Perkins Road, Sacramento, CA 95828, (916) 383-7387

Spca-Contra Costa County, 1865 Adobe Street, Concord, CA 94520, (925) 356-5669

Spca, 12910 Yukon Avenue, Hawthorne, CA 90250, (323) 678-2839

State Humane Associates, PO Box 299, Pacific Grove, CA 93950, (831) 647-8897

Supress Inc, 3655 Figueroa Street, Glendale, CA 91206, (818) 790-6383

Tri-Valley Animal Rescue, 4595 Gleason Drive, Pleasanton, CA 94588, (925) 803-7043

Tuolumne County Humane Society, 10040 Victoria Way, Jamestown, CA 95327, (209) 984-5489

Valley Humane Society, 273 Spring Street, Pleasanton, CA 94566, (925) 426-8656

Woods Humane Society, 4679 Broad Street, San Luis Obispo, CA 93401, (805) 543-9316

Yuba-Sutter SPCA Spay Clinic, 745 Sutter Street, Yuba City, CA 95991, (530) 673-6390

COLORADO

American Humane Association, 63 Inverness Drive East, Englewood, CO 80112, (303) 792-9900

Animal Welfare, 3420 West 8th Street, Pueblo, CO 81003 ,(719) 543-6464

Animal Welfare, 29129 Gale Road, Pueblo, CO 81006, (719) 543-6464

Ark Valley Humane Society, 28666 County Road 319, Buena Vista, CO 81211, (719) 395-2737

Boulder Valley Humane Society, 2323 55th Street, Boulder, CO 80301, (303) 442-4030

Colorado Humane Society, 2760 South Platte River Drive, Englewood, CO 80110, (303) 781-9344

Denver Dumb Friends League, 2080 South Quebec Street, Denver, CO 80231, (303) 671-5212

Eagle Valley Humane Society, 1400 Fairgrounds Road, Eagle, CO 81631, (970) 328-7387

Humane Society For Larimer, 6317 Kyle Avenue, Fort Collins, CO 80525, (970) 226-3647

Humane Society of Western Company, PO Box 502 ,Grand Junction, CO 81502, (970) 243-8823

Humane Society-Pikes Peak REG, 633 South 8th Street, Colorado Springs, CO 80905, (719) 473-1741

Humane Society-La Plata County, 1111 Camino Del Rio, Durango, CO 81301, (970) 259-2847

Intermountain Humane Society, 67318 US Highway 285, Bailey, CO 80421, (303) 838-2668

Longmont Humane Society, 9595 Nelson Road # G, Longmont, CO 80501, (303) 772-1232

Mile High Humane Society, 11470 York Street, Northglenn, CO 80233, (303) 452-2224

Pet Line 9, 2080 South Quebec Street, Denver, CO 80231, (303) 751-5557

Routt County Humane Society, 211 3rd, Steamboat Spgs, CO 80487, (970) 879-7247

Valley Humane League, PO Box 985, Alamosa, CO 81101, (719) 589-0703

CONNECTICUT

Animal Welfare Associates Inc, 161 Dunn Avenue, Stamford, CT 06905, (203) 322-8283

Connecticut Humane Society, 701 Russell Road, Newington, CT 06111, (860) 666-3337

Connecticut Humane Society, 169 Old Colchester Road, Quaker Hill, CT 06375, (860) 442-8583

Connecticut Humane Society, 788 Amity Road, Bethany, CT 06524, (203) 393-0150
Connecticut Humane Society , 455 Post Road East, Westport, CT 06880, (203) 336-4143

WASHINGTON, DC

Washington Animal Rescue League, 71 Oglethorpe Street NW, Washington, DC 20011, (202) 726-2556
Washington Humane Society, 7319 Georgia Avenue Northwest, Washington, DC 20012, (202) 723-5730

DELAWARE

Institute For The Dev-HMN RES, 655 South Bay Road, Dover, DE 19901, (302) 677-0687
Paws For Life Inc, 4466 Summit Bridge Road ,Middletown, DE 19709, (302) 376-7297

FLORIDA

Animal Rescue League Inc, 3200 North Military Trail, West Palm Beach, FL 33409, (561) 686-3663
Animal Rights Foundation of FL, 2300 W Sample Rd # 307, Pompano Beach, FL 33073, (954) 968-7622
Animal Shelter & Wildlife Soc, 5859 Avalon Road, Winter Garden, FL 34787, (407) 877-7387
Animal Welfare League Inc, 3519 Drance Street ,Port Charlotte, FL 33980, (941) 625-6720
Animals From The Ark Humane, 1103 W Hibiscus Blvd # 308X, Melbourne, FL 32901, (407) 757-9955
Big Dog Rescue, 1901 Faulk Drive, Tallahassee, FL 32303, (850) 562-3200
Border Collie Rescue, 886 State Road 26, Melrose, FL 32666, (352) 473-0100
Broward County Animal Care, 3100 NW 19th Terrace, Pompano Beach, FL 33064, (954) 970-0130
Broward County Animal Care, 1870 Southwest 39th Street, Fort Lauderdale, FL 33315, (954) 359-1313
Central Brevard Humane Society, 5100 W. Eau Gallie Boulevard, Melbourne, FL 32934, (407) 259-3400
Clay County Humane Society, 426 Blanding Boulevard, Orange Park, FL 32073, (904) 276-7729

Doberman Rescue Concern Inc, 325 Gardenia Street, West Palm Beach, FL 33401, (561) 659-1828

First Coast Humane Society, 995 Piper Lane, Fernandina Beach, FL 32034, (904) 261-0223

Flagler County Humane Society, 1 Shelter Drive, Palm Coast, FL 32137, (904) 445-1814

Gainesville Pet Rescue Inc, 1206 North Main Street, Gainesville, FL 32601, (352) 378-3606

Greyhound Adoption Leaque, 4128 Hibiscus Circle, West Palm Beach, FL 33409, (561) 615-0818

Halifax Humane Society, 2364 LPGA Boulevard, Daytona Beach, FL 32124, (904) 274-4703

Harmony Animal Hospital, 1401 West Indiantown Road, Jupiter, FL 33458, (561) 746-5501

Humane Society, Wiscon Road & Mobley, Brooksville, FL 34601, (352) 796-2711

Humane Society, 10699 Southwest 105th Avenue, Ocala, FL 34481, (352) 854-8230

Humane Society, 1665 Old Moultrie Road, St Augustine, FL 32086, (904) 829-2737

Humane Society of Tampa Bay, 3607 North Armenia Avenue, Tampa, FL 33607, (813) 876-7138

Humane Society of Vero Beach , 4701 41st Street, Vero Beach, FL 32967, (561) 567-2309

Humane Society of Treasure, 2675 Southeast Dixie Highway, Stuart, FL 34996 , (561) 287-5753

Humane Society of Lake County, 16435 McKinley Road, Umatilla, FL 32784, (352) 589-7400

Humane Society-Treasure Coast, 2018 Southeast Federal Highway, Stuart, FL 34994, (561) 286-6909

Humane Society-South Brevard, 2600 Otter Creek Lane, Melbourne, FL 32940, (407) 259-0601

Humane Society-Seminole County, 2800 County Home Road, Sanford, FL 32773, (407) 323-8685

Humane Society-Greater Miami, 2101 Northwest 95th Street, Miami, FL 33147, (305) 696-0800

Humane Society-Alachua County, 2029 Northwest 6th Street, Gainesville, FL 32609, (352) 373-5855

Humane Society-Collier County, 370 Airport Pulling Road North, Naples, FL 34104, (941) 643-1555

Humane Society-Sumter Company, 2899 County Rd 415, Lake Panasoffkee, FL 33538, (352) 793-9117

Humane Society-Broward County, 2070 Griffin Road, Fort Lauderdale, FL 33312, (954) 989-3977

Humane Society-Treasure Coast, 4100 SW Leighton Farm Ave, Palm City, FL 34990, (561) 223-8822

Humane Society-North America , 4880 West Colonial Drive, Orlando, FL 32808, (407) 523-7300

Jacksonville Humane Society, 8464 Beach Boulevard, Jacksonville, FL 32216, (904) 725-8768

Leesburg Humane Society, 41250 Emeralda Island Road, Leesburg, FL 34788, (352) 669-3312

Leon County Humane Society, 743 East Tennessee Street, Tallahassee, FL 32308, (850) 224-9193

National Greyhound Found., 8469 W Grover Cleveland Blvd, Homosassa, FL 34446, (352) 628-2281

Orlando Humane Society, 2727 Americana Boulevard, Orlando, FL 32839, (407) 351-7722

Osceola Animal Relief Inc, 21 Westchester Drive, Kissimmee, FL 34744, (407) 870-8082

Paws-2-Help Clinic, 500 25th Street, West Palm Beach, FL 33407, (561) 655-7572

Putnam County Humane Society, 112 Norma Street, Hollister, FL 32147 , (904) 325-1587

Safe Harbor Animal Rescue, 185 East Indiantown Road # 211, Jupiter, FL 33477, (561) 747-1598

Second Chance Ranch, 40643 Maggie Jones Road, Paisley, FL 32767, (352) 669-1116

Snap, 8464 Beach Boulevard, Jacksonville, FL 32216, (904) 725-8040

Society For Cruelty To Animals, 9075 Grant Street, Brooksville, FL 34613, (352) 596-7000

Spay-Neuter Clnic Eastside, 14365 East Colonial Drive, Orlando, FL 32826, (407) 207-8900

SPCA Adoption Center, 455 Cheney Highway, Titusville, FL 32780, (407) 269-0536

SPCA Animal Shelter, 2605 Flake Road, Titusville, FL 32796, (407) 267-8221

Suncoast Humane Society, 6781 San Casa Drive, Englewood, FL 34224, (941) 474-7884

Suwannee County Humane Society, 601 Houston Ave Northwest, Live Oak, FL 32060, (904) 364-5857

Tri County Humane Society, 584 Northwest 45 Drive, Delray Beach, FL 33445, (561) 496-6202

Upper Keys Humane SCTY, MM 101.5 Oceanside, Key Largo, FL 33037, (305) 451-3848

Volunteer Services For Animals, 7077 Airport Pulling Road North, Naples, FL 34109, (941) 597-4930

Rescue Rover!

GEORGIA

Animal Rescue Foundation, Milledgeville, GA 31061, (912) 454-1273

Atlanta Humane Society, 981 Howell Mill Road Northwest, Atlanta, GA 30318, (404) 875-5331

Augusta Humane Society Inc, 6 Milledge Road, Augusta, GA 30904, (706) 736-0186

Bartow County Humane Society, 1410 Burnt Hickory Road SW, Cartersville, GA 30120, (770) 383-3338

Berrien County Humane Society, 621 County Farm Road, Nashville, GA 31639, (912) 686-9113

Columbia County Humane Society, 4572 Waterford Drive, Evans, GA 30809, (706) 860-5020

Conyers-Rockdale Humane Soc, 1581 Loganville Highway NE, Conyers, GA 30012, (770) 922-4618

Dekalb Humane Society Inc, 5287 Covington Highway, Decatur, GA 30035, (770) 593-1155

Doraville Animal Control, 3883 Flowers Road, Atlanta, GA 30360, (770) 451-7845

Fayette County Humane Society, 849 Highway 74 South, Peachtree City, GA 30269, (770) 487-1073

Gilmer-Fannin Humane Society, Maxwell Road, Blue Ridge, GA 30513, (706) 632-7711

Humane Services Inc, 1550 Hardeman Avenue, Macon, GA 31201, (912) 745-4099

Humane Society, 7215 Sallie Mood Drive, Savannah, GA 31406, (912) 354-9515

Humane Society, Gil Harbin Industrial Boulevard, Valdosta, GA 31601, (912) 247-3266

Humane Society, 131 Chattin Drive, Holly Springs, GA 30142, (770) 345-6933

Humane Society of Hall County, 845 West Ridge Road, Gainesville, GA 30501

Humane Society-Griffin, 207 Laurel Street, Griffin, GA 30224, (770) 229-4925

Humane Society-North Georgia, 1170 Lewis Crump Road, Carnesville, GA 30521, (706) 384-3606

LA Grange Troup Humane Society, Aerotron PKWY, La Grange, GA 30240, (706) 882-0997

Muscogee County Humane Society, 7133 Sacerdote Lane, Columbus, GA 31907, (706) 563-3647

Newnan Coweta Humane Society , 41 Jefferson Street, Newnan, GA 30263, (770) 253-4694

Okefenokee Humane Society, 1501 Blackwell Street, Waycross, GA 31501, (912) 283-4214

Save-A-Life Animal Welfare, 4 Raintree Lane, Savannah, GA 31411, (912) 598-7729

Sumter Humane Society, 702 Magnolia Street, Americus, GA 31709,
(912) 924-0268
Thomaston Upson County Humane, 157 Wildwood Drive, Thomaston,
GA 30286, (706) 647-1881
TLC Humane Society, Dahlonega, GA 30533, (706) 864-2817

HAWAII

Hawaii Island Humane Society, Mamalahoa Highway, Kailua Kona, HI
96740, (808) 885-4558
Honolulu Zoological Society, 151 Kapahulu Avenue, Honolulu, HI
96815, (808) 926-3191
Kauai Humane Society, Lokokai Road, Hanapepe, HI 96716, (808)
335-5255
Kauai Humane Society, Salt Pond Road, Hanapepe, HI 96716, (808)
335-6000
Maui Humane Society, Mokulele Highway At MEHA MEHA Loop,
Puunene, HI 96784, (808) 877-3680
West Hawaii Humane Society Inc, PO Box 2695, Kailua Kona, HI
96745, (808) 329-8398

IOWA

Ames Animal Shelter, 325 Billy Sunday Road, Ames, IA 50010, (515)
239-5530
Animal Control of Cedar Rapids, 1401 Cedar Bend Lane, Ely, IA
52227, (319) 848-7373
Animal Lifeline of Iowa, 4989 Southeast 72nd Avenue, Carlisle, IA
50047, (515) 989-3473
Animal Protection Society-Iowa, 4340 East Oakwood Drive, Des
Moines, IA 50317, (515) 266-2005
Animal Protection League, PO Box 521, Burlington, IA 52601, (319)
753-2551
Animal Rescue League of Iowa, 5452 Northeast 22nd Street, Des
Moines, IA 50313, (515) 262-9503
Cedar Bend Humane Society, 1166 West Airline Highway, Waterloo,
IA 50703, (319) 232-6887
Des Moines County Humane SCTY, 2000 N Roosevelt Avenue,
Burlington, IA 52601, (319) 753-8389
Heartland Humane Society, 2603 Roemer Avenue, Ottumwa, IA
52501, (515) 682-1228
Humane Society, 7411 Mount Vernon Road Southeast, Cedar Rapids,
IA 52403, (319) 362-6288
Humane Society, 1206 North Jefferson Street, Indianola, IA 50125,
(515) 961-7080

Humane Society, 1473 Main Avenue, Clinton, IA 52732, (319) 242-2457

Humane Society of Scott County, 2134 West River Drive, Davenport, IA 52802, (319) 324-3960

Humane Society of Lucas Company, 118 East Lincoln Avenue, Chariton, IA 50049, (515) 774-5113

Humane Society of NW Iowa, 607 28th Street, Milford, IA 51351, (712) 338-2738

Jackson County Humane Society, RR 3, Maquoketa, IA 52060, (319) 652-5360

Knoxville Humane Society, 1293 160th Avenue, Knoxville, IA 50138, (515) 828-7387

Muscatine County Humane, 920 South Houser Street, Muscatine, IA, 52761, (319) 263-7358

North Central Human Service, 217 Maple Avenue, Nevada, IA 50201, (515) 382-6225

Sioux City Humane Society, 1665 18th Street, Sioux City, IA 51105, (712) 252-2614

Vinton Dog Pound, 5999 25th Street Drive, Vinton, IA 52349, (319) 472-4623

Washington County Humane, 1414 East Washington Street, Washington, IA 52353, (319) 653-6713

Webster County Humane Society, 2415 1/2 5th Avenue South, Fort Dodge, IA 50501, (515) 955-8343

IDAHO

Bonner Humane Society & Clinic, 900 Westwood Drive, Sandpoint, ID 83864, (208) 263-9282

Bonneville Humane Society, 444 North Eastern Avenue, Idaho Falls, ID 83402, (208) 529-9725

Humane Society of The Palouse, 19 White Avenue, Moscow, ID 83843, (208) 883-1166

Humane Society of Upper Valley, PO Box 51021, Idaho Falls, ID 83405, (208) 523-8888

Idaho Humane Society Spay Clinic, 4775 West Dorman Street, Boise, ID 83705, (208) 342-3599

Idaho Humane Society, 4775 West Dorman Street, Boise, ID 83705, (208) 342-3508

Kootenai Humane Society, Ramsey Road, Hayden Lake, ID 83835, (208) 772-4019

Lewis-Clark Animal Shelter, 1820 Shelter Road, Lewiston, ID 83501, (208) 746-1623

Pet Haven Humane Society, 333 West Orchard Avenue, Nampa, ID 83651, (208) 466-1298

Teton Valley Humane Society, 185 East 25 North, Driggs, ID 83422, (208) 354-3499

ILLINOIS

Animal Aid Humane Society, 527 15th Street, Moline, IL 61265, (309) 797-6550

Animal Care League, 1013 Garfield Street, Oak Park, IL 60304, (708) 848-8155

Animal Welfare League, 6224 South Wabash Avenue, Chicago, IL 60637, (773) 667-0088

Anti-Cruelty Society, 157 West Grand Avenue, Chicago, IL 60610, (312) 644-8338

Champaign County Humane Socity , 1911 East Main Street, Urbana, IL 61802, (217) 344-7297

Crawford County Humane Society, RR 2 Box 247, Robinson, IL 62454, (618) 544-8698

Elsa Wild Animal Appeal, 525 County Road 2550 North, Mahomet, IL 61853, (217) 897-1086

Five A Humane Society, 501 East Delmar Road, Alton, IL 62002, (618) 462-3721

Fox Valley Animal League, 600 South River Street, Aurora, IL 60506, (630) 892-9445

Geneseo Animal Control Center, 14606 ROOS Hill Road, Geneseo, IL 61254, (309) 944-4235

Hinsdale Humane Society, 22 North Elm Street, Hinsdale, IL 60521, (630) 323-5630

Humane Society , 14606 ROOS Hill Road, Geneseo, IL 61254, (309) 944-4868

Humane Society Decatur-Macon, 152 North Edward Street, Decatur, IL 62522, (217) 428-3058

Humane Society of Olney Area, Olney, IL 62450, (618) 392-2699

Humane Society of Carrol Count, Savanna, IL 61074, (815) 273-5331

Humane Society of Belleville, 1301 South 11th Street, Belleville, IL 62226, (618) 235-3712

Humane Society of Fulton Company, 43 South Main Street, Canton, IL 61520, (309) 647-5077

Humane Society-Mc Donough County , 1743 North Lafayette Street, Macomb, IL 61455, (309) 837-5611

Lake County Animal Protection , PO Box 106, Gurnee, IL 60031, (847) 740-3977

Mc Lean County Humane Society, 3001 Gill Street, Bloomington, IL 61704, (309) 664-7387

Midwest Greyhound Adoption , 6S031 Bliss Road, Sugar Grove, IL 60554, (630) 466-4022

Naperville Humane Society, 1620 West Diehl Road, Naperville, IL 60563, (630) 420-8989

Peoria Humane Society, 2606 North Knoxville Avenue, Peoria, IL 61604, (309) 682-9015

Pet Rescue Inc, 151 North Bloomingdale Road, Bloomingdale, IL 60108, (630) 893-0030

Plainfield Township Dog Pound, 1030 East Lockport Road, Plainfield, IL 60544, (815) 436-3250

Rescue A Golden Service, 5254 West Windsor Avenue, Chicago, IL 60630, (773) 777-5456

Rock Isle County Humane SCTY, 724 2nd Avenue West, Milan, IL 61264, (309) 787-6830

RTV Chicago, 474 Central Avenue, Highland Park, IL 60035, (847) 266-0068

Stephenson County Humane Soc, 59 East Monterey Street, Freeport, IL 61032, (815) 232-6164

Strays Halfway House Inc, Medinah, IL 60157, (630) 351-3150

Tree House Animal Foundation, 1212 West Carmen Avenue, Chicago, IL 60640, (773) 784-5488

Tri County Animal Protection , 613 River Lane, Dixon, IL 61021, (815) 288-7387

Wayne County Humane Society, 518 Southeast 4th Street, Fairfield, IL 62837, (618) 847-4012

Wildlife CPR, 5695 Hill Road, Decatur, IL 62522, (217) 963-6909

Will County Humane Society, 215 West SEIL Road, Joliet, IL 60431, (815) 741-0695

Winnebago County Animal Service, 4517 North Main Street, Rockford, IL 61103, (815) 877-3073

INDIANA

Animal Control Services, 5909 West Elliott, Wabash, IN 46992, (765) 563-5932

Animal Welfare League, 1100 Whitlock Avenue, Crawfordsville, IN 47933, (765) 362-8846

Animal Welfare Shelter, 1825 Chester Boulevard, Richmond, IN 47374, (765) 962-8393

Bartholomew County Humane Soc, 4110 East 200 South, Columbus, IN 47201, (812) 372-6063

Brown County Humane Society, 128 South State Road 135, Nashville, IN 47448, (812) 988-7362

Clay County Humane Society, 8280 North County Road 125 West, Brazil, IN 47834, (812) 446-5126

De Kalb Animal Shelter, 5221 US Highway 6, Butler, IN 46721, (219) 868-2409

Floyd County Animal Rescue, 37 West 5th Street, New Albany, IN 47150, (812) 949-9099

Friends of Animals, 550 North 350 West County Road, North Vernon, IN 47265, (812) 346-6799

Greene County Humane Society, Atlas Road, Linton, IN 47441, (812) 847-4780

Hamilton County Humane Society, 18102 Cumberland Road, Noblesville, IN 46060, (317) 773-4974

Hancock County Humane Society, 216 S Pennsylvania Street, Greenfield, IN 46140, (317) 462-5404

Hendricks County Humane Soc, 550 East Road, Brownsburg, IN 46112, (317) 852-4558

Humane Society, 1101 Buchanan Road, Evansville, IN 47720, (812) 426-2563

Humane Society, 1700 North 200 West, Angola, IN 46703, (219) 833-2877

Humane Society NW Indiana, 6800 East 7th Avenue, Gary, IN 46403, (219) 938-3339

Humane Society of Indianapolis, 7929 Michigan Rd Northwest, Indianapolis, IN 46268, (317) 872-5650

Humane Society of Noble County, 1305 Sherman Street, Kendallville, IN 46755, (219) 347-2563

Humane Society of Washington, West Joseph, Salem, IN 47167, (812) 883-4204

Humane Society of Hobart Inc, 2054 East State Road 130, Hobart, IN 46342, (219) 942-0103

Humane Society-Jackson Company, 1109 West Avenue G, Seymour, IN 47274, (812) 522-5200

Jay County Humane Society, 109 Sewer Plant Road, Portland, IN 47371, (219) 726-6339

Michiana Humane Society & SPCA, 722 Indiana Highway 212, Michigan City, IN 46360, (219) 872-4499

Monroe County Humane Assn, 3410 S. Old State Road 37, Bloomington, IN 47401, (812) 333-6242

Morgan County Humane Society, 690 West Mitchell Street, Martinsville, IN 46151, (765) 349-9177

Muncie Humane Society Inc, 4409 North Old State Road 3, Muncie, IN 47303, (765) 289-2585

Orange County Humane Society, 856 North Greenbriar Drive, Paoli, IN 47454, (812) 723-4142

Posey County Humane Society, 225 Steven Road, Mt Vernon, IN 47620, (812) 783-2001

Terre Haute Humane Society, 1811 South Fruitridge Avenue, Terre Haute, IN 47803, (812) 232-0293

Tippecanoe County Animal Shltr, 1705 South 2nd Street, Lafayette, IN 47905, (765) 474-5222

Regional Rescue Groups

Rescue Rover!

Tippecanoe County Humane SCTY, 1705 South 2nd Street, Lafayette
IN 47905, (765) 474-5222

White River Humane Society, 3511 Pumphouse Road, Bedford, IN
47421, (812) 279-2457

Wolfe Humane Society, Merrillville, IN 46410, (219) 985-1005

KANSAS

Animal Haven, 9800 West 67th Street, Shawnee Mission, KS 66203,
(913) 432-7548

AWOL Humane Society, 116 South 23rd Street, Independence, KS
67301, (316) 331-7931

Caring Hands Humane Society , 1400 Southeast 3rd Street, Newton,
KS 67114, (316) 283-0839

Ford County Humane Society, 207 Gunsmoke Street, Dodge City, KS
67801, (316) 225-1481

Heart of Jackson Humane Soc , PO Box 126, Holton, KS 66436, (785)
364-5156

Helping Hands Humane Society, 2625 Northwest Rochester Road,
Topeka, KS 66617, (785) 233-7325

Humane Association of Saline County, PO Box 1544, Salina, KS 67402,
(785) 825-6652

Humane Society, 1120 Commercial Street, Emporia, KS 66801, (316)
342-4477

Humane Society, 104 North 6th Street, Atchison, KS 66002, (913) 367-
3647

Humane Society of Kansas City, 316 Minnesota Avenue, Kansas City,
KS 66101, (913) 371-3869

Humane Society of Miami County, PO Box 136, Paola, KS 66071, (913)
294-8400

Humane Society of Se Kansas, 485 East 560th Avenue, Pittsburg, KS
66762, (316) 232-1840

Hutchinson Humane Society, 3501 Stewart Street, Hutchinson, KS
67502, (316) 662-6981

Leavenworth Animal Welfare Soc , 857 Sherman Avenue,
Leavenworth, KS 66048, (913) 651-5297

Martin B Peck Animal Shelter, 230 West 19th Street, Ottawa, KS 66067,
(785) 242-2967

Pratt County Humane Society, 1402 West 1st Street, Pratt, KS 67124,
(316) 672-6777

Riley County Humane Society, 821 Wildcat RDG, Manhattan, KS 66502,
(785) 776-8433

KENTUCKY

Fund For Animals Inc, 233 West Broadway, Louisville, KY 40202, (502) 587-0508

Greenup County Humane Society, 2135 Argillite Road, Flatwoods, KY 41139, (606) 836-7529

Greyhound Adoption-Kentuckiana, 10912 Pineview Court, Jeffersontown, KY 40299, (502) 266-9582

Greyhound Pets of America, 7406 Wesboro Road, Louisville, KY 40242, (502) 339-7004

Greyhound Pets of America, 6409 South Drive, Valley Station, KY 40272, (502) 995-3767

Greyhound Rescue & Adoption , PO Box 99913, Louisville, KY 40269, (502) 493-0457

Humane Society Inc of Danville, 777 North Danville Bypass, Danville, KY 40422, (606) 238-1117

Humane Society of Calloway CTY, 212 Barnett Street, Hazel, KY 42049, (502) 492-8838

Humane Society-Nelson County, 2391 New Haven Road, Bardstown, KY 40004, (502) 349-2082

Kentucky Humane Society, 241 Steedley Drive, Louisville, KY 40214, (502) 366-3355

Lawrence County Humane Society, Isaac Branch Road, Louisa, KY 41230, (606) 673-4509

Leslie County Humane Society, Wendover Street, Wendover, KY 41775, (606) 279-4803

Mercer County Humane Society, 896 Moberly Road, Harrodsburg, KY 40330, (606) 734-5154

Pike County Humane Society, 120 Cedar Drive, Pikeville, KY 41501, (606) 437-7992

Scott County Humane Society, PO Box 821, Georgetown, KY 40324, (502) 863-3279

Shelby County Humane Society, 1600 Locust Grove Road, Shelbyville, KY 40065, (502) 633-4033

LOUISANA

Capital Area Animal Welfare, 6357 QUIN Drive, Baton Rouge, LA 70817, (225) 752-5801

Greyhound Pets of America, 106 Pine Oak Drive, Covington, LA 70433, (504) 893-0966

Humane Society, 1314 Troy Road, New Iberia, LA 70560, (318) 365-1923

Humane Society of Central LA, 100 Sadie Lane, Pineville, LA 71360, (318) 641-8855

Rescue Rover!

Jefferson SPCA, 1 Humane Way, New Orleans, LA 70123, (504) 733-7387

Louisiana SPCA Animal Clinic, 1319 Japonica Street, New Orleans, LA 70117, (504) 944-7445

Ouachita Humane Society Inc, 920 Freight Drive, Monroe, LA 71203, (318) 387-9553

River Cities Humane Society, 4695 Construction Avenue, Monroe, LA 71203, (318) 387-4392

St Tammany Humane Society, 20384 Harrison Avenue, Covington, LA 70433, (504) 892-7387

MASSACHUSETTS

Animal Rescue League of Boston, 10 Chandler Street, Boston, MA 02116, (617) 426-9170

Animal Rescue League, 358 Highland Avenue, Salem, MA 01970, (978) 744-7910

Canine Connections, Norwood, MA 02062, (781) 440-0477

Framingham Animal Humane Soc , 30 Pond Street, Ashland, MA 01721, (508) 875-3776

Friends of The Plymouth Pound, Plymouth, MA 02360, (508) 224-6651

Mass Humane Society, 79 Milk Street # 912, Boston, MA 02109, (617) 542-7661

Mass Society, Pittsfield, MA 01201, (413) 448-6046

Neponset Valley Humane Society, Stoughton, MA 02072, (781) 341-2675

MARYLAND

Animal Welfare Society, 33 1/2 Queen Street, Cumberland, MD 21502, (301) 724-0446

Calvert Animal Welfare League, PO Box 350, St Leonard, MD 20685, (410) 586-0555

Humane Society of Dorchester, 4930 Bucktown Road, Cambridge, MD 21613, (410) 228-3090

Humane Society of Charles County, 71 Industrial Park Drive, Waldorf, MD 20602, (301) 645-8181

Montgomery County Humane SCTY, 14645 Rothgeb Drive, Rockville, MD 20850, (301) 279-1823

Wicomico County Humane Society, 5130 Citation Drive, Salisbury, MD 21804, (410) 749-7603

William Snyder Foundation Inc, 3600 Clipper Mill Road, Baltimore, MD 21211, (410) 366-0787

Worcester County Humane SCTY, Eaglenest Road, Ocean City, MD 21842, (410) 213-0146

MAINE

Greater Androscoggin Humane Society, 420 Poland Spring Road, Auburn, ME 04210, (207) 783-2311

Paws Animal Welfare, RR 3 Box 845, St Francis, ME 04774, (207) 398-3511

MICHIGAN

Al-Van Humane Society, 73303 8th Avenue, South Haven, MI 49090, (616) 637-5062

Animal Aid, PO Box 851, Brighton, MI 48116, (810) 231-4497

Animal Protective Association, 214 South Dwight Street, Jackson, MI 49203, (517) 784-6063

Animal Shelter of Alger County, 510 East Munising Avenue, Munising, MI 49862, (906) 387-4131

Associated Wildlife Educators, 2515 Gatzke Road, Cedar, MI 49621, (616) 228-2900

Cascades Humane Society, 626 North Mechanic Street, Jackson, MI 49202, (517) 788-6587

Cheboygan County Humane Soc, 1536 Hackelburg Road, Cheboygan, MI 49721, (616) 238-8221

Clare County Animal Shelter, 4040 Hazel Road, Harrison, MI 48625, (517) 539-3221

Copper Country Humane Society, 115 South 41st Street, Houghton, MI 49931, (906) 487-9560

Cruelty Investigation Division, 7401 Chrysler Drive, Detroit, MI 48211, (313) 872-3401

Genesee County Humane Society, G3325 South DORT Highway, Burton, MI 48529, (810) 744-0511

Humane Shelter, 3881 Tripp Road, Osseo, MI 49266, (517) 523-2308

Humane Society, 1890 Bristol Avenue Northwest, Grand Rapids, MI 49504, (616) 453-7757

Humane Society, 6266 Lapeer Road, North Street, MI 48049, (810) 987-4357

Humane Society, 3201 LA Franier Road, Traverse City, MI 49686, (616) 946-5116

Humane Society of Macomb, 11350 22 Mile Road, Shelby Twp, MI 48317, (810) 731-9210

Humane Society of Huron Valley, 3100 Cherry Hill Road, Ann Arbor, MI 48105, (734) 662-4365

Humane Society & Animal Rescue, 640 Marquette Avenue, Muskegon, MI 49442, (616) 773-8689

Humane Society of Livingston, PO Box 351, Brighton, MI 48116, (810) 229-7640

Rescue Rover!

Humane Society of Monroe, 833 North Telegraph Road, Monroe, MI
48162, (734) 243-3669

Humane Society of Bay County, 207 South Linn Street, Bay City, MI
48706, (517) 893-0451

Humane Society of Saginaw, 123 South Niagara Street, Saginaw, MI
48602, (517) 797-2482

Humane Society of Barry County, Hastings, MI 49058, (616) 945-0602

Humane Society-Calhoun Area, 2500 Watkins Road, Battle Creek, MI
49015, (616) 963-1796

Huron Humane Society, 3510 Woodward Avenue, Alpena, MI 49707,
(517) 356-4794

Kalamazoo Humane Society, 4239 South Westnedge Avenue,
Kalamazoo, MI 49008, (616) 345-1181

Lenawee Humane Society, 705 West Beecher Street, Adrian, MI
49221, (517) 263-9111

Little Traverse Bay Humane, 2070 North US Highway 31, Petoskey, MI
49770, (616) 347-2396

Marquette County Humane SCTY, 84 Snowfield Road, Negaunee, MI
49866, (906) 475-6661

Michigan Animal Adoption NTWK, 37720 Amrhein Road, Livonia, MI
48150, (734) 462-2111

Michigan Anti-Cruelty Society, 13569 Joseph Campau Street, Detroit, MI
48212, (313) 891-7188

Michigan Humane Society, 3600 Auburn Road, Auburn Hills, MI 48326,
(248) 852-7420

Michigan Humane Society, 7401 Chrysler Drive, Detroit, MI 48211,
(313) 872-3400

Michigan Humane Society Center, 37255 Marquette Street, Westland,
MI 48185, (734) 721-7300

Missaukee Humane Society, Lake City, MI 49651, (616) 839-3800

Newaygo County Humane Society, 78 North Webster Street, White
Cloud, MI 49349, (616) 689-1867

Ottawa Shores Humane Society, 7982 West Olive Road, West Olive,
MI 49460, (616) 399-2119

Peninsula Animal Welfare Soc, Sault Sainte Marie, MI 49783, (906)
632-2287

Pet Hot Line, 505 Leelanau Avenue, Frankfort, MI 49635, (616) 352-
4647

Sanilac County Humane Society, 6565 Lakeshore Road, Lexington, MI
48450, (810) 359-2307

Shiawassee Humane Society, 2752 West Bennington Road, Owosso,
MI 48867, (517) 723-4262

Wonderland Humane Society, 1406 6th Avenue, Cadillac, MI 49601,
(616) 775-6400

MINNESOTA

Animal Allies Humane Society, 407 1/2 West Michigan Street, Duluth, MN 55802, (218) 722-5341

Animal Ark, 2600 Industrial Court, Hastings, MN 55033, (651) 438-9195

Animal Ark Thrift & Pet Store, 809 7th Street East, St Paul, MN 55106, (651) 772-8983

Animal Humane Society, 845 Meadow Lane North, Golden Valley, MN 55422, 612) 522-4325

Animal Sanctuary of St. Croix Valley, st Office Box 847, Stillwater, MN 55082, 651) 223-4734

Becker County Humane Society, Box 1506, Detroit Lakes, MN 56502, 18) 847-0511

Beltrami Humane Society, 21 Bemidji Avenue North, Bemidji, MN 56601, (218) 751-7910

Blue Earth Nicollet County, 517 East Madison Avenue, Mankato, MN 56001, (507) 625-6373

Brown County Humane Society, New Ulm, MN 56073, (507) 359-2312

Friends-Animals Humane Society, 1003 Cloquet Avenue, Cloquet, MN 55720, (218) 879-1655

Goodhue County Humane Society, 1213 Brick Avenue, Red Wing, MN 55066, (651) 388-5286

Heartland Animal Rescue Team, 1401 Danielson Road North, Brainerd, MN 56401, (218) 829-4141

Hibbing Animal Shelter, 12825 Old Highway 169, Hibbing, MN 55746, (218) 778-6468

Humane Society of Lyon County, 800 Kossuth Avenue, Marshall, MN 56258, (507) 537-0803

Humane Society Animal Shelter, 720 East Robert Street, Crookston, MN 56716, (218) 281-7225

Humane Society-Freeborn County, Albert Lea, MN 56007, (507) 377-8501

Humane Society-Ramsey County, 1115 Beulah Lane, St Paul, MN 55108, (651) 645-7387

Humane Society-Wright County, 8875 Highway 12, Delano, MN 55328, (612) 972-3577

Humane Society-Kandiyohi County, 1804 Trott Avenue Southwest, Willmar, MN 56201, (320) 235-7612

Isle Area Humane Society, 320 Main Street West, Isle, MN 56342, (320) 676-3499

Lake County Humane Society, PO Box 27, Two Harbors, MN 55616, (218) 834-5806

Lake Superior Humane Society, 112 Waterfront Drive, Two Harbors, MN 55616, (218) 834-3966

Lakes Area Humane Society, 801 Sanstead Street East, Garfield, MN 56332, (320) 834-2219

Mesabi Humane Society, 2305 Southern Drive, Virginia, MN 55792, (218) 741-7425

Minnesota Federated Humane, 33 10th Avenue South # 110, Hopkins, MN 55343, (612) 935-1846

Minnesota Humane Society, 1885 University Avenue West, St Paul, MN 55104, (651) 645-1344

Minnesota Valley Humane SCTY, 1313 Highway 13 East, Burnsville, MN 55337, (612) 894-5000

Mower County Humane Society, Austin, MN 55912, (507) 437-9262

North Metro Humane Society, 1411 Main Street Northwest, Coon Rapids, MN 55448, (612) 754-1642

Ottertail Humane Society, 1933 West Fir Avenue, Fergus Falls, MN 56537, (218) 739-3494

Rice County Humane Society, 1201 Cannon Circle, Faribault, MN 55021, (507) 334-7117

Steele County Humane Society, 511 North Cedar Avenue, Owatonna, MN 55060, (507) 451-4512

Waseca County Humane Society, 17324 408th Avenue, Waseca, MN 56093, (507) 835-4272

Winona Area Humane Society, 57 East 3rd Street, Winona, MN 55987, (507) 452-3135

MISSOURI

Animal Protective Association, 1705 South Hanley Road, St Louis, MO 63144, (314) 645-4610

Callaway County Humane Society, 2019 Westminster Avenue, Fulton, MO 65251, (573) 642-7483

Carthage Humane Society Inc, 13887 Cedar Road, Carthage, MO 64836, (417) 358-6402

Caruthersville Humane Shelter, 302 West 3rd Street, Caruthersville, MO 63830, (573) 333-0100

Dent County Animal Shelter , East Highway 32, Salem, MO 65560, (573) 729-3556

Franklin County Humane Society, 1222 West Main Street, Union, MO 63084, (314) 583-4300

Humane Society, PO Box 36, St Joseph, MO 64502, (816) 232-6955

Humane Society of Missouri, 1201 Macklind Avenue, St Louis, MO 63110, (314) 647-8800

Humane Society of US, 306 East 12th Street # 625, Kansas City, MO 64106, (816) 474-0888

Humane Society of Missouri, 2400 Drilling Service Drive, Maryland Heights, MO 63043, (314) 647-8800

Humane Society of St Charles, 1099 Pralle Lane, St Charles, MO 63303, (314) 949-9918

Joplin Humane Society, Swede Lane, Webb City, MO 64870, (417) 623-3642

Missouri Wildlife Rescue Center, 203 Ramsey Lane Rear, Ballwin, MO 63021, (314) 394-1880

National Society For Animals, 7611 State Line Road, Kansas City, MO 64114, (816) 523-0500

New Nodaway Humane Society, Highway 136, Maryville, MO 64468, (660) 582-7337

Northeast Missouri Humane Soc, 29 & Lily, Hannibal, MO 63401, (573) 221-9222

P A LS of Lincoln Company, Troy, MO 63379, (314) 528-6286

People For Animal Rights, 12821 Grandview Road, Grandview, MO 64030, (816) 767-1199

Polk County Humane Society, 1805 East Broadway Street, Bolivar, MO 65613, (417) 777-3647

Southwest Missouri Humane Soc, 3161 West Norton Road, Springfield, MO 65803, (417) 833-2526

St Louis Regap, PO Box 25383, St Louis, MO 63125, (314) 894-0834

Tri Company Humane Society, 745 East Springfield Street, St James, MO 65559, (573) 265-7955

Wayside Waifs Inc, 3901 East 119th Street, Kansas City, MO 64137, (816) 761-8151

MISSISSIPPI

Amory Humane Society, 1317 Old Highway 6, Amory, MS 38821, (601) 256-7566

Humane Society Natchez Adams, 392 Liberty Road, Natchez, MS 39120, (601) 442-4001

Humane Society Columbus13 Airline Road, Columbus, MS 39702, (601) 327-3107

Humane Society-S Mississippi, 13756 Washington Avenue, Gulfport, MS 39503, (228) 863-3354

Mississippi Animal Rescue, 4395 South Drive, Jackson, MS 39209, (601) 969-1631

Vicksburg Warren Humane SCTY, 6600 Highway 61 South, Vicksburg, MS 39180, (601) 636-6631

Wildlife Rehabilitation SCTY, 23228 Woodland Way, Pass Christian, MS 39571, (228) 452-9453

MONTANA

Animal Welfare League, 910 6th Avenue, Laurel, MT 59044, (406) 628-6019

Bitter Root Humane Associates, 262 Fairgrounds Road, Hamilton, MT 59840, (406) 363-5311

Humane Society of Park County, PO Box 705, Livingston, MT 59047, (406) 222-2111

Humane Society Animal Shelter, 2125 North Rouse Avenue, Bozeman, MT 59715, (406) 587-0456

Northwest Montana Humane Soc, 43 Woodland Park Drive # 10, Kalispell, MT 59901, (406) 752-7297

Pet Assistance League, Northwest of Lewistown, Lewistown, MT 59457, (406) 538-2990

Silver Bow Humane Society, 699 Centennial Avenue, Butte, MT 59701, (406) 782-8450

NORTH CAROLINA

Animal Haven, 3927 Bragg Boulevard, Fayetteville, NC 28303, (910) 864-9040

Animal Protection Society, 606 North Main Street, Roxboro, NC 27573, (336) 597-5013

Avery County Humane Society, 1824 Stamey Branch Road, Newland, NC 28657, (828) 733-6312

Buncombe County Animal Shelter, 72 Lees Creek Road, Asheville, NC 28806, (828) 253-6807

Cashiers Area Humane Society, 200 Gable Road, Cashiers, NC 28717, (828) 743-5752

Chatham Humane Society, Pittsboro, NC 27312 , (919) 542-5757

Cleveland County Humane SCTY, 1010 West Sumter Street, Shelby, NC 28150, (704) 484-0019

Colonial Capital Humane, PO Box 326, New Bern, NC 28563, (252) 633-0146

County Animal Shelter, Ross Road, Brevard, NC 28712, (828) 883-3713

Craven Pamlico Animal Service Center , 620 Lagoon Road, New Bern, NC 28562, (252) 637-4606

Foster Animal Network, 107 Church Road, Asheville, NC 28804, (828) 236-2287

Greyhound Friends of NC, 2908 Oak Ridge Road, Oak Ridge, NC 27310, (336) 643-0233

Haywood Animal Welfare Association, 201 West Main Street, Hazelwood, NC 28786, (828) 456-9976

Humane Alliance of WNC, 702 Riverside Drive, Asheville, NC 28801, (828) 252-2079

Humane Soc, 1815 Park Dr, Charlotte, NC 28204, (704) 377-1714
Humane Soc, 108 Hamilton Rd, Lexington,NC 27295, (336) 248-2706
Humane Soc, 2700 Toomey Ave,Charlotte,NC 28203,(704) 377-0534
Humane Soc, PO Box 1552, Henderson, NC 27536, (252) 492-5211
Humane Soc, 61 Miller St, Winston Salem,NC 27104,(336) 721-1303
Humane Society of Rowan County, 112 West Innes Street, Salisbury,
  NC 28144, (704) 636-5700
Humane Society of Concord, 1008 Litchfield Place, Concord, NC
  28027, (704) 784-4434
Humane Society of Randolph, 902 Straight Street, Asheboro, NC
  27203, (336) 629-7387
Humane Society of Rutherford, PO Box 998, Rutherfordton, NC
  28139, (828) 286-0222
Humane Society of Beaufort, PO Box 8, Washington, NC 27889,
  (252) 946-1591
Humane Soc of Edgecombe, Nashville, NC 27856, (252) 446-1669
Humane Society of Halifax County, 54 Dog Pound Road, Halifax, NC
  27839, (252) 583-7387
Iredell County Humane Society, 317 Camelot Drive, Statesville, NC
  28625, (704) 871-2594
Macon County Humane Society, 851 Lake Emory Road, Franklin, NC
  28734, (828) 524-4588
Mitchell County Animal Rescue, 308 Highway 19E, Spruce Pine, NC
  28777, (828) 765-6952
North Carolina Society-Prvntn, 500 Blue Ridge Road, Black Mountain,
  NC 28711, (828) 669-2296
Pitt County Humane Society, 2850 East Firetower Road, Greenville,
  NC 27858, (252) 756-1268
Rockingham Humane Soc, Wentworth, NC 27375, (336) 349-4379
SPCA,3911 Presbyterian Rd,Greensboro,NC 27406, (336) 697-9399
Watauga County Humane Society, 200 Casey Lane, Boone, NC
  28607, (828) 264-7865

NORTH DAKOTA

Central Dakota Humane Society, 2090 37th Street, Mandan, ND
  58554, (701) 667-2020
Humane Soc, 1201 28th Ave North,Fargo,ND 58102,(701) 239-0077
Humane Society of Grand Forks, 6900 Gateway Drive, Grand Forks,
  ND 58203, (701) 775-3732
Souris Valley Humane Society, 1935 20th Avenue Southeast, Minot,
  ND 58701, (701) 852-6133

Rescue Rover!

NEBRASKA

Aurora Humane Soc, 1301 23rd St, Aurora, NE 68818,(402) 694-2738
Capital Humane Society, 2320 Park Boulevard, Lincoln, NE 68502,
    (402) 477-7722
Central Nebraska Humane Soc, 1312 Sky Park Road, Grand Island, NE
    68801, (308) 385-5305
Dodge County Humane Society, 787 South Luther Road, Fremont, NE
    68025, (402) 721-3282
Mc Cook Humane Society, 100 South Street, Mc Cook, NE 69001,
    (308) 345-2372
Nebraska HS, 8801 Fort St, Omaha, NE 68134,(402) 444-7800
Panhandle Humane Society, 126 South Beltline Highway West,
    Scottsbluff, NE 69361, (308) 635-0922
Town & Country Humane Society, 14110 South 84th Street, Papillion,
    NE 68046, (402) 339-5355

NEW HAMPSHIRE

Greater Derry HS, 57 Lawrence Rd, Derry, NH 03038,(603) 894-4385
Humane Society of New England, 24 Ferry Road, Nashua, NH 03060,
    (603) 889-2275
Lancaster Humane Society, 564 Martin Meadow Pond Road,
    Lancaster, NH 03584, (603) 788-4500
SPCA, 130 Washington Street, Concord, NH 03303, (603) 753-6751
Staples Veterinary Clinic, West Claremont Road, Claremont, NH 03743,
    (603) 542-4531
Upper Valley Humane Society, Old Route 10, Enfield, NH 03748, (603)
    448-1878

NEW JERSEY

Animal Rescue Force, 290 State Route 18, East Brunswick, NJ 08816,
    (732) 257-7559
Animal Rescue Force, 90 Wilson Avenue, Englishtown, NJ 07726,
    (732) 792-8101
Animal Welfare Association, 509 Gibbsboro Marlton Road, Kirkwood
    Vrhes, NJ 08043, (609) 424-2288
Closter Animal Welfare Society, 231 Herbert Avenue, Closter, NJ
    07624, (201) 768-0200
Gloucester County SPCA, Ogden Road, Swedesboro, NJ 08085,
    (609) 467-0182
Humane Society of Bergen County, 154 Park Avenue, East
    Rutherford, NJ 07073, (201) 896-9300
Humane Society US Mid-Atlntc, 270 US Highway 206 # 4, Flanders,
    NJ 07836, (973) 927-5611

Paws Inc Animal Shelter, 77 North Willow Street, Montclair, NJ 07042, (973) 746-5212

People For Animals,433 Hillside Ave, Hillside,NJ 07205,(908) 964-6887

Plainfield Humane Society, 75 Rock Avenue, Plainfield, NJ 07063, (908) 754-0300

Salem County Humane Society, Game Creek Road, Carneys Point, NJ 08069, (609) 299-2220

Society To Protect Animals, 1059 West Route 40, Carneys Point, NJ 08069, (609) 299-1155

St Huber's Giralda Animal Hospital, 3201 US Highway 22, North Branch, NJ 08876, (908) 526-3330

Warren County SPCA, 228 Main Street, Hackettstown, NJ 07840, (908) 813-1990

Warren Hills Animal Society, 88 West Stewart Street, Washington, NJ 07882, (908) 689-4425

NEW MEXICO

Animal Humane Assn-New Mexico, 615 Virginia Street SE, Albuquerque, NM 87108, (505) 255-5523

Dona Ana County Humane Society, 4711 North Main Street, Las Cruces, NM 88012, (505) 382-0018

Humane Society, 4 Industrial Park, Deming, NM 88030,(505) 546-2024

Humane Society Kennels, 703 East McGaffey Street, Roswell, NM 88201, (505) 622-8950

Humane Society-Lincoln County, Gavilan Canyon Road, Ruidoso, NM 88345, (505) 257-9841

Lea County Humane Society, 1018 1/2 West Alabama Street, Hobbs, NM 88242, (505) 392-4638

Mc Kinley County Humane Soc, North US Highway 666, Gallup, NM 87301, (505) 863-2616

Paws Santa Fe, PO Box 704, Pecos, NM 87552, (505) 471-3708

San Juan Animal League, 3609 North Sunset Avenue, Farmington, NM 87401, (505) 325-3366

Sangre DE Cristo Animal Prtctn, 102 West San Francisco Street, Santa Fe, NM 87501, (505) 983-2200

NEVADA

Betty Honn's Animal Adoption, 1442 Bermuda Road, Henderson, NV 89014, (702) 361-2484

Nevada Humane Society, 200 Kresge Lane, Sparks, NV 89431, (775) 331-5770

Pahrump Humane Society, 1451 East Highway 372, Pahrump, NV 89048, (775) 727-6203

Rescue Rover!

Pershing County Humane Society, 700 South Meridian Road, Lovelock, NV 89419, (775) 273-7297

NEW YORK

Adirondack Humane Society Inc, 14 Margaret Street, Plattsburgh, NY 12901, (518) 561-7876

Allegany Cty SPCA, Route 19, Wellsville, NY 14895, (716) 593-2200

Animal Defense League Inc, 11 State Street, Pittsford, NY 14534, (716) 218-9555

Animal Protective Foundation, 53 Maple Avenue, Scotia, NY 12302, (518) 374-3944

Animal Rights Advocates-WNY, Hamburg, NY 14075, (716) 648-6423

Buffalo Greyhound Adoption Inc, 149 Keller Avenue, Kenmore, NY 14217, (716) 873-1165

Chemung County Humane Society, 2435 State Route 352, Elmira, NY 14903, (607) 732-1827

Columbia-Greene Humane Society, Route 385, Athens, NY 12015, (518) 945-1286

Hamburg Eden Animal Res.,Lackawanna,NY 14218,(716) 821-1915

Humane Society, 5664 Horatio St, Utica, NY 13502, (315) 738-4357

Humane Society At Lollypop FRM, 99 Victor Road, Fairport, NY 14450, (716) 223-1330

Humane Society of Walden Inc, 2489 Albany Post Road, Walden, NY 12586, (914) 778-5115

Humane Society Mowawk & Hudson, Oakland Avenue, Albany, NY 12204, (518) 434-8128

Humane Society of Wayne County, 1475 County House Road, Lyons, NY 14489, (315) 946-3389

Humane Society-Batavia, 9 Vernon Avenue, Batavia, NY 14020, (716) 343-7722

Humane Wildlife Control, 245 East Boyds Road, Carmel, NY 10512, (914) 764-4154

I Speak, PO Box 207, Old Bethpage, NY 11804, (516) 938-6376

James A Brennan Memorial Soc, 437 Nine Mile Tree Road, Gloversville, NY 12078, (518) 725-0115

League For Animal Protection, 104 Deposit Road, East Northport, NY 11731, (516) 757-4517

Massena Humane Society Inc, South Racket River Road, Massena, NY 13662, (315) 764-1330

Paws Animal,3371 Gaines Basin Rd, Albion,NY 14411,(716) 589-6397

Paws Animal Welfare Society, 217 Oak Street, Bellmore, NY 11710, (516) 364-7297

Pet Pride of New York Inc, 9 West Main St, Honeoye Falls, NY 14472, (716) 582-1088

Potsdam Animal Shelter, 17 Madrid Avenue, Potsdam, NY 13676, (315) 265-3199

Save Our Strays, PO Box 21286,Brooklyn, NY 11202,(718) 332-3956

Scottsville Veterinary Hospital, 3750 Scottsville Road, Scottsville, NY 14546, (716) 889-8340

Services For The Underserved, 394 Bristol Street # A, Brooklyn, NY 11212, (718) 342-1640

Skip of NY, 545 Madison Ave, New York, NY 10022, (212) 538-9166

Society For The Prevention, 205 Ensminger Road, Tonawanda, NY 14150, (716) 875-7360

SPCA, 1640 Hanshaw Road, Ithaca, NY 14850, (607) 257-1822

United Jewish Appeal, 155 Washington Avenue # 303, Albany, NY 12210, (518) 436-1091

Wanderers Rest Humane Association Inc, 1 Southland Drive, Canastota, NY 13032, (315) 697-2796

OHIO

Animal Protective League, 1729 Willey Avenue, Cleveland, OH 44113, (216) 771-4616

Animal Rescue Fund Inc, 85 Lucy Run Road, Amelia, OH 45102, (513) 753-9252

Animal Rights Community, 6304 Cary Avenue, Cincinnati, OH 45224, (513) 542-6810

Ashland County Humane Society, 1710 Garfield Avenue, Ashland, OH 44805, (419) 289-1455

Belmont County Dog Shelter , 45244 National Road West, St Clairsville, OH 43950, (740) 695-4708

Carrollton City Humane Society, 1128 Antigua Road Southwest, Carrollton, OH 44615, (330) 627-3044

Citizens For Humane Action, 5505 Westerville Road Rear, Westerville, OH 43081, (614) 891-5280

Cleveland Animal Life Line, 23102 Beachwood Boulevard, Cleveland, OH 44122, (216) 382-7387

Concerned Citizens for Animal Welfare, 389 Liberty Street, Conneaut, OH 44030, (440) 593-6004

Crawford County Humane Society, 3590 State Route 98, Bucyrus, OH 44820, (419) 562-9149

Fayette County Humane Society, 113 1/2 South Main St, Washington Ct Hs, OH 43160, (740) 335-8126

Friends of Pets, 2780 Fallen Log Ln, Akron,OH 44333,(330) 864-7387

Fulton County Humane Society, 109 Beech Street, Wauseon, OH 43567, (419) 335-9009

Geauga County Humane Society, 12513 Merritt Drive, Chardon, OH 44024, (440) 285-9440

Homeward Bound Humane Society, 548 Dog Leg Road, Heath, OH 43056, (740) 323-2100

Humane Society, 5201 Urbana Road, Springfield, OH 45502, (937) 399-2917

Humane Society, 1823 Spring Lane, Portsmouth, OH 45662, (740) 353-5517

Humane Society of Greene County, 765 North Detroit Street, Xenia, OH 45385, (937) 376-3001

Humane Society of Hancock County, 4550 Fostoria Avenue, Findlay, OH 45840, (419) 423-1664

Humane Society of Erie County, 1911 Superior Street, Sandusky, OH 44870, (419) 626-6220

Humane Society of Akron, 4904 Quick Road, Peninsula, OH 44264, (330) 657-2010

Humane Society of Sandusky Inc, 108 Arch Street, Fremont, OH 43420, (419) 334-4517

Humane Society of Ottawa County, 2424 East Sand Road, Port Clinton, OH 43452 (419) 734-5191

Humane Society & Spay Neuter, 4920 State Route 37 East, Delaware, OH 43015, (740) 369-7387

Humane Society-Guernsey County, 62800 Bennett Avenue, Cambridge, OH 43725, (740) 439-1903

Humane Society-Capital Area, 3015 Scioto Darby Executive Court, Hilliard, OH 43026, (614) 777-7387

Humane Society-Greater Dayton, 1661 Nicholas Road, Dayton, OH 45418, (937) 268-7387

Humane Society-United States, 745 Haskins Road # G, Bowling Green, OH 43402, (419) 352-5141

Humane Society-Auglaize County, Keller Drive, Wapakoneta, OH 45895, (419) 738-7808

Knox County Humane Society, 729 Columbus Road, Mt Vernon, OH 43050, (740) 392-2287

Lake County Humane Society, 7564 Tyler Boulevard # East, Mentor, OH 44060, (440) 951-6122

Lake Erie Greyhound Rescue Inc, 278 North Broadway, Geneva, OH 44041, (440) 466-1347

Lancaster Fairfield Humane Soc, 1983 East Main Street, Lancaster, OH 43130, (740) 687-0627

Lima-Allen County Humane Soc, 1125 South Seriff Road, Lima, OH 45805, (419) 991-1775

Mahoning County Humane Society, 2801 Market Street, Youngstown, OH 44507, (330) 782-4071

Medina County SPCA, 790 Lafayette Road, Medina, OH 44256, (330) 723-7722

Meigs County Humane Society, 305 North 2nd Avenue, Middleport, OH 45760, (740) 992-6064

Rescue Rover!

Miami County Humane Society, 1190 North County Road 25A, Troy, OH 45373, (937) 335-9955

Morgan County Humane Society, 1625 Mill Street, Chesterhill, OH 43728, (740) 554-5831

Morrow County Humane, Mount Gilead, OH 43338, (419) 947-5791

North Coast Humane Society, 269 Shoregate Mall, Willowick, OH 44095, (440) 585-5155

Ohio Humane Education Association, PO Box 546, Grove City, OH 43123, (614) 875-1810

Paws Adoption Center Inc, 2790 Cincinnati Dayton Road, Middletown, OH 45044, (513) 422-7297

Paws Animal Shelter, 1535 West US Highway 36, Urbana, OH 43078, (937) 653-6233

Pet Guards Shelter,290 W Ave,Tallmadge, OH 44278, (330) 849-0634

SavAPet,4434 Westerville Rd, Columbus, OH 43231, (614) 478-9313

Seneca County Humane Society, 925 North Water Street, Tiffin, OH 44883, (419) 447-5704

Shelby County Humane Society, 227 East Court Street, Sidney, OH 45365, (937) 498-9462

Sicsa Pet Adoption Center, 2600 Wilmington Pike, Dayton, OH 45419, (937) 294-6505

SPCA Hamilton County, 3949 Colerain Avenue, Cincinnati, OH 45223, (513) 541-6100

Toledo Humane Society, 1920 Indian Wood Circle, Maumee, OH 43537, (419) 891-0705

Toledo Humane Society, 5660 Southwyck Boulevard, Toledo, OH 43614, (419) 867-3440

Wood County Humane Society, 801 Van Camp Road, Bowling Green, OH 43402, (419) 352-7339

Wyandot Cty Humane Soc, 9640 County Highway 330, Upper Sandusky, OH 43351, (419) 294-4477

OKLAHOMA

Animal Aid of Tulsa Inc, 1412 South Harvard Avenue, Tulsa, OK 74112, (918) 493-3321

Animal Rescue Foundation, 4945 East 41st Street, Tulsa, OK 74135, (918) 622-5962

Bryan County Humane Society, 3625 South 9th Avenue, Durant, OK 74701, (580) 924-5873

C-S Animal Control & Adoption, Snyder, OK 73566, (580) 569-4038

Humane Assn, PO Box 10772, Enid, OK 73706, (580) 234-6793

Humane Society of Grove, 64301 East 290 Road, Grove, OK 74344, (918) 786-7630

Humane Society of Stillwater, 1710 South Main Street, Stillwater, OK 74074, (405) 377-1701

Pets & People Humane Society, 501 Ash Avenue, Yukon, OK 73099, (405) 350-7387

Promoting Animal Welfare Soc., PO Box 1525, Muskogee, OK 74402, (918) 686-7297

Rogers County Humane Society, PO Box 1046, Claremore, OK 74018, (918) 341-9126

Tulsa Society For Prevention, 2910 Mohawk Boulevard, Tulsa, OK 74110, (918) 428-2529

Volunteers-Animal Welfare Inc, 9228 North May Avenue, Oklahoma City, OK 73120, (405) 842-6772

OREGON

Animal Rescue-SPCA, PO Box 5045, Grants Pass, OR 97527, (541) 479-1910

Blue Mountain Humane Associates, 3212 Highway 30, La Grande, OR 97850, (541) 963-0807

Calling All Pets Inc, 1035 Rogue River Highway, Gold Hill, OR 97525, (541) 855-7301

Central Coast Humane Society, 831 Northeast Yaquina Heights Dr, Newport, OR 97365, (541) 265-3719

Columbia Humane Society, 2084 Oregon Street, St Helens, OR 97051, (503) 397-4353

Committed Alliance To Strays, 104 North Ross Lane, Medford, OR 97501, (541) 779-2916

County of Wasco Animal Shelter, 200 River Road, The Dalles, OR 97058, (541) 296-5189

Evergreen-Doe Humane Society, 10605 Southeast Loop Road, Dayton, OR 97114, (503) 472-0341

Florence Area Humane Society, 2840 North Rhododendron Dr, Florence, OR 97439, (541) 997-4277

Heartland Humane Society, 5311 Southwest Airport Place, Corvallis, OR 97333, (541) 757-9000

Humane Society, 2910 Table Rock Road, Medford, OR 97501, (541) 779-3215

Humane Society of Redmond, 925 Southeast Sisters Avenue, Redmond, OR 97756, (541) 923-0882

Humane Society of The Ochocos, 394 North Belknap Street, Prineville, OR 97754, (541) 447-7178

Humane Society of Prineville, 2086 Northwest Oneill Highway, Prineville, OR 97754, (541) 416-0168

Humane Society-The Willamette, 4246 Turner Road Southeast, Salem, OR 97301, (503) 585-5900

Humane Society-Cottage Grove, 2555 Mosby Creek Road, Cottage Grove, OR 97424, (541) 942-3130

Humane Society-Central Oregon, 61170 27th Street, Bend, OR 97702, (541) 382-3537

Jefferson County Kennels, 1694 Southeast McTaggart Road, Madras, OR 97741, (541) 475-6889

Klamath Humane Society Inc, 831 Main Street, Klamath Falls, OR 97601, (541) 884-8319

Klamath Humane Society, 500 Miller Island Road, Klamath Falls, OR 97603, (541) 882-1119

Oregon Humane Society SPCA, 1067 Northeast Columbia Blvd, Portland, OR 97211, (503) 285-7722

Predator Defense Institute, Post Office Box 5079, Eugene, OR 97405, (541) 937-4261

Rogue Valley Humane Society, 1169 Redwood Avenue # A, Grants Pass, OR 97527, (541) 479-5154

Safe Haven Humane Society, 33071 Highway 34 Southeast, Albany, OR 97321, (541) 928-2789

South Coast Animal League, PO Box 1232, Coos Bay, OR 97420, (541) 347-6888

South Coast Humane Society, 620 Hemlock Street, Brookings, OR 97415, (541) 412-0325

SPCA Information, Roseburg, OR 97470, (541) 957-2107

PENNSYLVANIA

Animal Friends, 2643 Penn Avenue, Pittsburgh, PA 15222, (412) 566-2103

Bradford County Humane Society, US Route 220, Ulster, PA 18850, (570) 888-2114

Butler County Humane Society, 1002 Evans City Road, Renfrew, PA 16053, (724) 789-1150

Cumberland Valley Shelter, 2325 Country Road, Chambersburg, PA 17201, (717) 263-5791

Going Home Greyhounds, 181 Spruce Haven Drive, Wexford, PA 15090, (724) 935-6298

Green Acres Sanctuary, 2867 Copper Kettle Highway, Rockwood, PA 15557, (814) 926-4902

Humane League, 2195 Lincoln Highway East, Lancaster, PA 17602, (717) 393-6551

Humane Society, RR 2, Franklin, PA 16323, (814) 677-4040

Humane Society of Greene County, RR 3 Box 96A, Waynesburg, PA 15370, (724) 627-9988

Humane Society of Cambria Company, 188 Airport Road, Johnstown, PA 15902, (814) 535-6116

Humane Society of Indiana Cty, Indiana, PA 15701, (724) 465-7387
Humane Society of Mercer Cty, Sharon, PA 16146, (724) 981-5445
Humane Society of Westmoreland, 804 Green Street, Greensburg, PA 15601, (724) 837-3779
Humane Society-Bedford County, 511 East Penn Street, Bedford, PA 15522, (814) 623-8968
Huntingdon County Humane Soc, RR 3 Box 218A, Huntingdon, PA 16652, (814) 643-7387
Lawrence County Humane Society, Pearson Mill Road, New Castle, PA 16101, (724) 654-8520
Make Peace With Animals, PO Box 488, New Hope, PA 18938, (215) 862-0605
Pawsfree, PO Box 108, Wexford, PA 15090, (724) 774-3764
Penna SPCA, 2801 Bloom Road, Danville, PA 17821, (570) 275-0340

RHODE ISLAND

Pals Humane Society Gift Shop, 49 Cedar Swamp Road, Smithfield, RI 02917, (401) 231-7580

SOUTH CAROLINA

Anderson County Humane Society, 5030 White City Park Road, Anderson, SC 29625, (864) 225-9855
Animal Adoption League of York, PO Box 2453, Rock Hill, SC 29732, (803) 325-8282
Concerned Citizens For Animals, 3627 Fork Shoals Road, Simpsonville, SC 29680, (864) 243-4222
Florence Area Humane Society, 1007 Stockade Drive, Florence, SC 29506, (843) 669-2921
Grand Strand Humane Soc, 3241 10th Ave Extension North, Myrtle Beach, SC 29577, (843) 448-9151
Grand Strand Humane Society, 409 Bay Street, North Myrtle Bch, SC 29582 , (843) 249-4948
Greenville Humane Society, 328 Furman Hall Road, Greenville, SC 29609, (864) 242-3626
Hilton Head Island Humane Association, 10 Humane Way, Hilton Head Isle, SC 29926, (843) 681-8686
Humane Society of York County, 2596 Cherry Road, Rock Hill, SC 29732, (803) 325-2050
Humane Society of Grandstrand, 3241 10th Ave Extension N, Myrtle Beach, SC 29577, (843) 448-5891
Humane Society-Prevention, 121 Humane Lane, Columbia, SC 29209, (803) 783-1267

Lancaster Cty Humane Soc., Lancaster, SC 29720, (803) 283-1833
SPCA Animal Shelter, 3861 Leeds Avenue, Charleston, SC 29405, (843) 747-4849
SPCA Humane Organization , 1140 South Guignard Drive, Sumter, SC 29150, (803) 773-9292
St Frances Humane Society, Ridge Road, Georgetown, SC 29440, (843) 546-0780

SOUTH DAKOTA

Aberdeen Area Humane Society, 13452 385th Avenue, Aberdeen, SD 57401, (605) 226-1200
Beadle County Humane Society, 5063 Dakota Avenue South, Huron, SD 57350, (605) 352-8955
Heart of the Earth Marketing, 205 High, Fruitdale, SD 57742, (605) 892-0154
Humane Animal Shelter, 1305 6th Avenue Northwest, Watertown, SD 57201, (605) 882-2247
Jo Anne Jewell's Precious Gems, PO Box 5643, Rapid City, SD 57709, (605) 348-1635
Sioux Falls Area Humane Soc, 2001 North 3rd Avenue, Sioux Falls, SD 57104, (605) 338-4441
South Dakota Animal Welfare, PO Box 178, Sioux Falls, SD 57101, (605) 339-0785

TENNESSEE

Bristol Humane Soc, PO Box 1586, Bristol, TN 37621, (423) 968-9136
Cannon Cty Animal Humane, Woodbury, TN 37190, (615) 464-6010
Cheatman Animal Awareness, 115 Annabelle Way, Ashland City, TN 37015, (615) 792-7283
Happy Tales Humane, PO Box 680446, Franklin, TN 37068, (615) 791-0827
Humane Educational Society, 212 N Highland Park Ave, Chattanooga, TN 37404, (423) 622-8913
Humane Society, 325 South Church Avenue, Dyersburg, TN 38024, (901) 285-4889
Humane Society of Cumberland, East Lane, Crossville, TN 38555, (931) 484-9700
Humane Society of Sumner County, 16 Volunteer Drive, Hendersonville, TN 37075, (615) 822-0061
Humane Society Clarksville, 119 Providence Boulevard, Clarksville, TN 37042, (931) 648-8042
Humane Society-Coffee County, 707 South Washington Street, Tullahoma, TN 37388, (931) 728-8036

Humane Society, 410 Eno Road, Dickson, TN 37055, (615) 446-7387
Humane Society-The TN Valley, 1000 North Central Street, Knoxville, TN 37917, (423) 594-1455
Jackson Madison County Humane, 3107 Paul Coffman Drive, Jackson, TN 38301, (901) 422-5366
Knox County Humane Society, 800 Millwood Road, Knoxville, TN 37920, (423) 573-9674
Knoxville Police Animal Cntrl, 800 Millwood Road, Knoxville, TN 37920, (423) 521-1297
Loudon County Animal Shelter, 480 Rock Quarry Road, Loudon, TN 37774, (423) 458-5593
Love At First Sight Pet Center, 4423 Murphy Road, Nashville, TN 37209, (615) 297-2464
McMinn Regional Humane Society, 219 Alford Street, Athens, TN 37303, (423) 744-9548
Memphis Humane Society, 2238 Central Avenue, Memphis, TN 38104, (901) 272-1753
Nashville Humane Association, 112 Harding Place, Nashville, TN 37205, (615) 352-4030
Precious Friends Puppy Rescue, 114 Kraft Street # H, Clarksville, TN 37040, (931) 551-4407
Sullivan County Humane Society, 621 Industry Drive, Kingsport, TN 37660, (423) 247-1671
Union County Humane Society, Maynardville, TN 37807, (423) 992-7969
Warren County Humane Society, 94 Collie Drive, Mc Minnville, TN 37110, (931) 473-5720
Your Volunteer Humane Society, 571 Little Notchey Creek Rd, Madisonville, TN 37354, (423) 420-0009

TEXAS

Alpine Humane Society, 309 West SUL Ross Avenue, Alpine, TX 79830, (915) 837-2532
Amarillo SPCA,Rockwell Road, Canyon, TX 79015, (806) 655-4336
Amarillo-Panhandle Humane SCTY, 3501 South Osage Street, Amarillo, TX 79118, (806) 373-1716
Animal Aid Humane Society, 1533 Wooded Acres Drive, Waco, TX 76710, (254) 776-7303
Animal Connection of Texas, 6541 Stichter Street, Dallas, TX 75230, (214) 373-7867
Animal Control, 504 North Queen Street, Palestine, TX 75801, (903) 731-8443
Animal Defense League, 11300 Nacogdoches Road, San Antonio, TX 78217, (210) 655-1481

Animal Rescue Shelter Inc, 12500 South Washington Street, Amarillo,
  TX 79118, (806) 622-1082
Animal Shelter, 805 Woodlawn Ave, Jacksonville, TX 75766, (903)
  586-9723
Animal Shelter, 1225 West Freeway Street, Grand Prairie, TX 75051,
  (972) 660-4269
Animal Shelter, 2032 Circle Road, Waco, TX 76706, (254) 754-1454
Arlington Humane Society Inc, 7817 South Cooper Street, Arlington,
  TX 76001, (817) 468-0444
Big Spring Humane Society, West Interstate 20, Big Spring, TX 79720,
  (915) 267-7832
Bulverde Area Humane Society, PO Box 50, Bulverde, TX 78163,
  (830) 438-7387
Citizens For Animal Protection, 11923 Katy Freeway, Houston, TX
  77079, (281) 497-0534
Cooke County Humane Society, PO Box 543, Gainesville, TX 76241,
  (940) 668-6309
Denton Humane Soc, PO Box 1972, Denton,TX 76202,(940) 382-7387
Donald G Austin Memorial Animal SH, 2007 Old Chappell Hill Rd,
  Brenham, TX 77833, (409) 277-1277
Ector County Humane Society, 1902 North County Road West,
  Odessa, TX 79763, (915) 337-7387
Freeman-Fritts Animal Shelter , 515 Spur 100, Kerrville, TX 78028,
  (830) 257-4500
Fund For Animals, PO Box 70286,Houston, TX 77270, (713) 862-3863
Guadalupe County Humane Soc, 2484 North State Highway 46,
  Seguin, TX 78155, (830) 372-2055
Gulf Coast Humane Society, 3118 Cabaniss Road, Corpus Christi, TX
  78415, (361) 225-0845
Hill Country Animal League, 115 West Bandera Road, Boerne, TX
  78006, (830) 249-8040
Hill Country Greyhound Adptn, 430 Flint Rock Lane, Seguin, TX 78155,
  (830) 303-2229
Hill Country Humane Society, 1007 Avenue K, Marble Falls, TX 78654,
  (830) 693-7387
Houston Humane Society, 14700 Almeda Road, Houston, TX 77053,
  (713) 433-6421
Houston SPCA, 900 Portway Dr, Houston,TX 77024,(713) 869-7722
Humane Association-Lamar County, 3342 Northeast Loop 286, Paris,
  TX 75460, (903) 784-6774
Humane Society, 1845 North Expressway, Brownsville, TX 78520,
  (956) 544-0414
Humane Society, 7203 Skillman Street # 106, Dallas, TX 75231, (214)
  343-3666
Humane Society of SE Texas, 2050 Spindletop Ave, Beaumont, TX
  77705, (409) 833-0504

Humane Society of Montgomery, 1016 East Dallas Street, Conroe, TX 77301, (409) 756-3914

Humane Society Upper Valley, 1/4 M East McCall-On-Trenton Road, McAllen, TX 78504, (956) 686-1141

Humane Society of Dallas County, 2719 Manor Way, Dallas, TX 75235, (214) 350-7387

Humane Soc Adoption, 580 Maple,McKinney,TX 75069,(972) 562-4357

Humane Society of Harlingen, 1106 Markowsky Avenue, Harlingen, TX 78550, (956) 425-7297

Humane Soc, 3016 Milam Dr, Brownwood, TX 76801, (915) 646-0617

Humane Society of Nacogdoches, 507 East Hospital Street, Nacogdoches, TX 75961, (409) 569-7272

Humane Society of Bexar County, 307 West Jones Avenue, San Antonio, TX 78215, (210) 226-7461

Humane Society of North Texas, 1840 East Lancaster Avenue, Fort Worth, TX 76103, (817) 332-5367

Humane Society of El Paso Inc, 325 Shelter Place, El Paso, TX 79905, (915) 532-6971

Humane Society Permian Basin, 3917 West Wall Street, Midland, TX 79703, (915) 689-0999

Humane Society of Kerrville, 1327 Junction Highway, Kerrville, TX 78028, (830) 895-2701

Humane Society-Spca Austin, 124 West Anderson Lane, Austin, TX 78752, (512) 837-7985

Humane Society-Tom Green County, 805 North BAZE Street, San Angelo, TX 76903, (915) 653-8056

Humane Society-Navarro, 617 South 12th Street, Corsicana, TX 75110, (903) 654-4928

Humane Society-Greater Dallas, 5408 East Grand Avenue, Dallas, TX 75223, (214) 824-1663

Johnson County Humane Society, 7680 Floyd Hampton Road, Crowley, TX 76036, (817) 297-1511

Low Cost Spay & Neuter Program, PO Box 72064, Corpus Christi, TX 78472, (361) 991-7124

Lubbock Animal Service, 401 North Ash Avenue, Lubbock, TX 79403, (806) 767-2057

Man & Beast Inc, 3918 Naco Perrin Boulevard # 109, San Antonio, TX 78217, (210) 590-7387

Metroport HS, PO Box 701, Roanoke, TX 76262, (817) 491-9499

Mid-Cities Humane Society, PO Box 540493, Grand Prairie, TX 75054, (972) 263-4567

Palestine An. Shtr,333 Armory Rd,Palestine,TX 75801,(903) 729-8074

Pet Rescue Society Inc, 739 West Mansfield Highway, Kennedale, TX 76060, (817) 572-3220

Plainview Humane Society, 500 East 3rd Street, Plainview, TX 79072, (806) 296-2311

Shelby County HS 1318 Louisiana St, Center,TX 75935,(409) 590-9030
Six Flags HS, 305 Rebel Street, Victoria, TX 77904, (361) 575-8573
SPCA, 506 Interchange St, McKinney, TX 75069, (972) 562-7387
SPCA of Texas,362 South Industrial Boulevard, Dallas, TX 75207, (214) 651-9611
SPCA Pet Clinic, 15 Kerry Road, Midland, TX 79706, (915) 684-7582
SPCA Pick Up Service, 3507 Shepherd Lane, Mesquite, TX 75180, (972) 557-0105
Special Pals, 3830 Greenhse Rd,Houston,TX 77084,(281) 579-7387
Taylor-Jones Humane Society, 3811 North 1st Street, Abilene, TX 79603, (915) 672-7124
Texas Cares, 18504 Featherwood Dr, Dallas,TX 75252,(972) 985-3858
Texas Federation-Humane, 124 West Anderson Lane, Austin, TX 78752, (512) 837-0879
Williamson County Humane Soc, 2121 North Mays Street, Round Rock, TX 78664, (512) 244-9247
Winnie Berry Pet Adoption Center, 1102 North John Redditt Drive, Lufkin, TX 75904, (409) 639-1880

UTAH

Best Friends Animal Sanctuary, 5001 Angel Canyon Rd, Kanab, UT 84741
Humane Society of Utah, 4242 South 300 West, Murray, UT 84107, (801) 261-2919
Wasatch Humane, 880 S 500 W, Bountiful, UT 84010, (801) 299-8508

VIRGINIA

Alleghany Humane Society, 304 Karnes Road, Lowmoor, VA 24457, (540) 862-2436
Animal Assistance League, 1149 New Mill Drive, Chesapeake, VA 23322, (757) 548-0045
Animal Care, Main St, Mathews, VA 23109, (804) 725-5242
Animal Welfare League Inc, 107 South Main Street, Kilmarnock, VA 22482, (804) 435-0822
Bedford Humane Society Inc, Bedford, VA 24523, (540) 586-6100
Campbell County Humane Society, Route 29, Rustburg, VA 24588, (804) 821-4416
Colonial Beach HS, Colonial Beach, VA 22443, (804) 224-2122
Gloucester-Mathews Humane Soc, 9131 Rangtang Road, Gloucester, VA 23061, (804) 693-5520

Humane Society of Shenandoah, 341 Landfill Road, Edinburg, VA 22824, (540) 984-8955

Humane Society of Fairfax County, 4057 Chain Bridge Road, Fairfax, VA 22030, (703) 385-7387

Isle of Wight Humane Society, 14076 Carrollton Boulevard, Carrollton, VA 23314, (757) 238-2852

Lend-A-Paw Relief Organization, 320 King Street, Alexandria, VA 22314, (703) 706-3003

Lynchburg Humane Society, 3305 Naval Reserve Road, Lynchburg, VA 24501, (804) 846-1438

Middleburg Humane Fnd,Rte 622 Marshall,VA 20115,(540) 364-3272

National Humane Education Soc, 521 East Market Street # A, Leesburg, VA 20176, (703) 777-8319

Norfolk SPCA, 916 Ballentine Boulevard, Norfolk, VA 23504, (757) 622-3319

Portsmouth Humane Society, 2704 Frederick Boulevard, Portsmouth, VA 23704, (757) 397-6004

Potomac Animal Allies Inc, Independent Hill, Manassas, VA 20110, (703) 791-2900

Pulaski County Humane Society, Dublin, VA 24084, (540) 674-0089

Rappahannock Animal Welfare, Route 639, Amissville, VA 20106, (540) 937-3283

Rappahannock Humane Society, P.O. Box 8313, Fredericksburg, VA 22404, (540) 785-1470

Society For Prevention-Cruelty, 1523 William Street, Fredericksburg, VA 22401, (540) 373-9008

SPCA Humane Society, 523 J Clyde Morris Boulevard, Newport News, VA 23601, (757) 595-1399

SPCA of Virginia Beach, 3040 Holland Road, Virginia Beach, VA 23456, (757) 427-0070

St Francis Humane Association, 3620 Luckylee Crescent, Richmond, VA 23234, (804) 598-6636

Tidewater Humane Inc, 4604 Pembroke Lake Circle, Virginia Beach, VA 23455, (757) 497-7729

VERMONT

Bennington County Humane Soc, PO Box 620, Shaftsbury, VT 05262, (802) 375-2898

Green Mountain Humane Society, PO Box 1426, White River Jct, VT 05001, (802) 296-7297

Humane Society-United States, Route 112, Jacksonville, VT 05342, (802) 368-2790

Lucy Mackenzie Humane Society, Cox District Road, Woodstock, VT 05091, (802) 457-3080

Springfield Humane Society, 399 Skitchewaug Trail, Springfield, VT 05156, (802) 885-3997

Windham County Humane Society, 916 West River Road, Brattleboro, VT 05301, (802) 254-2232

WASHINGTON

Alternative Humane Society, PO Box 2321, Bellingham, WA 98227, (360) 671-7445

Animal Control & Pet Licensing, 2521 North Flora Road, Spokane, WA 99216, (509) 458-2532

Animal Foster Care Association, Omak, WA 98841, (509) 826-2227

Animal Protection Society, 993 Shelter Road, Friday Harbor, WA 98250, (360) 378-2158

Animal Protection Society, Eastsound, WA 98245, (360) 376-6777

Animal Rescue & Adoption, 8737 Whitewood Loop Southeast, Yelm, WA 98597, (360) 458-3281

Animal Rescue Families, PO Box 165, Bremerton, WA 98337, (360) 698-6576

Blue Mountain Humane Society, C Street At Airport, Walla Walla, WA 99362, (509) 525-2452

Clallam County Humane Society, 272 West Highway 101, Port Angeles, WA 98363, (360) 452-5226

Clallam County Humane Society, 2105 West Highway 101, Port Angeles, WA 98363, (360) 457-8206

Dog Patch Group Inc, 2287B Marble Valley Basin Road, Colville, WA 99114, (509) 684-5433

Humane Soc, 1312 S 18th Ave, Pasco, WA 99301, (509) 545-9301

Humane Society Spokane, 6607 North Havana Street, Spokane, WA 99217, (509) 467-5235

Humane Society For Tacoma, 2608 South Center Street, Tacoma, WA 98409, (253) 383-2733

Humane Society Shelter, 2405 Birchfield Road, Yakima, WA 98901, (509) 457-6854

Humane Society-Cowlitz County, 11 Fibre Way, Longview, WA 98632, (360) 577-0151

Humane Society-Skagit Valley, 1641 Kelleher Road, Burlington, WA 98233, (360) 757-0445

Kitsap Humane Society, 9167 Dickey Road Northwest, Silverdale, WA 98383, (360) 692-6977

Moses Lake-Grant County Humane, 7321 Randolph Road NE, Moses Lake, WA 98837, (509) 762-9616

Noah Animal Shelter, 160 Can KU Road # North, Stanwood, WA 98292, (360) 387-9797

Northwest Animal Rights Ntwrk, 1704 East Galer Street, Seattle, WA 98112, (206) 323-7301

Regional Rescue Groups

Paws, 15305 44th Ave West, Lynnwood, WA 98037, (425) 787-250(
Paws of Bainbridge Island, PO Box 10811, Bainbridge Isle, WA 98110,
  (206) 842-2451
Paws, PO Box 2235, Bremerton, WA 98310, (360) 613-1050
Paws of Bremerton Adoption, 2207 East 11th Street, Bremerton, WA
  98310, (360) 373-7043
Petsavers/Arf, PO Box 5118, Bremerton, WA 98312, (360) 692-8304
Spokanimal Care, 710 N Napa St,Spokane,WA 99202,(509) 534-8133
SW Washington Humane Society, 2323 West 26th Extension,
  Vancouver, WA 98660, (360) 693-4746
Wenatchee Valley Humane Soc., 1474 S Wenatchee Avenue,
  Wenatchee, WA 98801, (509) 662-9577
Whidbey Animals Improvement, 20168 State Route 20, Coupeville, WA
  98239, (360) 678-3722
Whidbey Animals Improvement, 6115 Main Street, Freeland, WA 98249,
  (360) 331-2818

WISCONSIN

Adams County Animal Shelter, 1982 11th Avenue, Friendship, WI
  53934, (608) 339-6700
Animal Protective League Inc, 2130 North 106th Street, Milwaukee, WI
  53226, (414) 453-7177
Animal Welfare Shelter, 951 County Road G, Neenah, WI 54956, (920)
  722-9544
Associated Society/Animal, 318 Grove Street, Sparta, WI 54656 ,
  (608) 269-3525
Bay Area Humane Society, 1830 Radisson Street, Green Bay, WI
  54302, (920) 469-3110
Beaver Dam Humane Society Inc, 210 Stoddart Street, Beaver Dam, WI
  53916, (920) 887-7447
Chippewa County Humane Assn, 10503 County Hwy S, Chippewa
  Falls, WI 54729, (715) 382-4832
Clark County Humane Society, W3926 State Highway 73, Neillsville, WI
  54456, (715) 743-4550
Coulee Region Humane Society, 2850 Larson Street, La Crosse, WI
  54603, (608) 781-4014
Countryside Humane Society, 2706 Chicory Road, Racine, WI 53403,
  (414) 554-6699
Eau Claire County Human Associates, 3800 Old Town Hall Road, Eau
  Claire, WI 54701, (715) 839-4747
Elmbrook Humane Society Inc, 21210 Enterprise Avenue, Brookfield,
  WI, 53045, (414) 782-9261
Forest County Humane Society, 8322 County Road DD, Pickerel, WI
  54465, (715) 484-7603

Fox Valley Humane Association, 3401 West Brewster Street, Appleton, WI, 54914, (920) 733-1717

Green County Humane Society, 1500 7th Avenue, Monroe, WI 53566, (608) 325-9600

Happy Puppies Inc, 27700 Highway 80 South, Richland Center, WI 53581, (608) 647-3753

Hope Safehouse, 1911 Taylor Avenue, Racine, WI 53403, (414) 634-4571

Humane Animal Welfare Society, 701 Northview Road, Waukesha, WI 53188, (414) 542-8851

Humane Society , 2250 Pennsylvania Avenue, Madison, WI, 53704, (608) 246-3340

Humane Society, 1541 Boomer Street, Watertown, WI 53094, (920) 261-1270

Humane Society, N8128 State Road 65, River Falls, WI 54022, (715) 426-5535

Humane Society Dunn County, 302 Brickyard Road, Menomonie, WI 54751, (715) 232-9790

Humane Society Inc , PO Box 512, Stevens Point, WI 54481, (715) 344-6012

Humane Society of Douglas County, 3302 S Humane Society Rd, Range, WI 54874, (715) 398-6784

Humane Society-Barron County, 1571 Guy Street, Barron, WI 54812, (715) 537-9063

Juneau County Humane Society, N8537 State Road 58, New Lisbon, WI, 53950, (608) 565-2313

Langlade County Humane Society, 2204 Clermont Street, Antigo, WI 54409, (715) 627-4333

Lincoln County Humane Society, 200 North Memorial Drive, Merrill, WI 54452, (715) 536-3459

Northwoods Humane Society, PO Box 82, Hayward, WI 54843, (715) 634-5394

Oshkosh Area Humane Society, 815 Dempsey Trail, Oshkosh, WI 54901, (920) 424-2128

Ozaukee Humane Society Inc, 2073 Highway West, Grafton, WI 53024, (414) 377-7580

Protect Animal Life Inc, 1413 Wyoming Way, Madison, WI 53704, (608) 249-4156

Puppyland Humane Society Inc, 3456 County Road D, West Bend, WI 53090, (414) 338-3369

Sauk County Humane Society, PO Box 257, Baraboo, WI 53913, (608) 356-2520

Shady Acres Animal Shelter, 623 East Shady Lane, Neenah, WI 54956, (920) 725-0002

Shawano County Humane Society, 1010 Airport Drive, Shawano, WI 54166, (715) 526-2606

Regional Rescue Groups

Sheboygan County Humane Soc, 3107 North 20th Street, Sheboygan, WI 53083, (920) 458-2012

Standard Retirement Foundation, 8465 Carr Factory Road, Cuba City, WI 53807, (608) 744-7337

Washburn County Humane Society, W9315 Woodyard Road, Shell Lake, WI54871, (715) 468-4200

Washington County Humane Soc, 3650 Highway 60, Slinger, WI 53086, (414) 677-4388

Wisconsin Humane Society, 4151 North Humboldt Boulevard, Milwaukee, WI 53212, (414) 961-0310

WEST VIRGINIA

Animal Welfare Society, PO Box 147, Charles Town, WV 25414, (304) 725-0589

Greenbrier County Humane SCTY, 205 North Court Street, Lewisburg, WV 24901, (304) 645-4775

Humane Society-Morgan County, 4100 Valley Road, Berkeley Springs, WV 25411, (304) 258-5592

Humane Society-Harrison County, Saltwell Road, Shinnston, WV 26431, (304) 592-1600

Kanawha Action For Animals Inc, 806 Greenbrier Street, Charleston, WV 25311, (304) 342-7297

Kanawha Charleston Humane Association, 1248 Greenbrier St, Charleston, WV 25311, (304) 342-1576

Monongalia County Humane SCTY, 235 High Street # 401, Morgantown, WV 26505, (304) 296-6247

Putnam County Humane Society, 3983 Teays Valley Road, Hurricane, WV 25526, (304) 757-3571

Randolph County Humane Society, Weese Street Extension, Elkins, WV 26241, (304) 636-7844

Upshur County Humane Society, Mud Lick Road, Buckhannon, WV 26201, (304) 472-8741

WYOMING

Fund For Animals Inc, PO Box 11294, Jackson, WY 83002, (307) 859-8840

Humane Society, PO Box 502, Gillette, WY 82717, (307) 682-7465

Humane Society, 260 Crescent Drive, Casper, WY 82604, (307) 265-5439

Humane Society of Park County, 2630 Highway 120, Cody, WY 82414, (307) 587-5110

Rock Springs Humane Society, 310 Yellowstone Road, Rock Springs, WY 82901, (307) 362-1636

Weston County Humane Society , 115 Cambria, Newcastle, WY 82701 , (307) 746-9770

Regional Rescue Groups

Part 5:

Group Updates and
Order Forms

Updates & Order Forms

Rescue Group &
Humane Society Update

Please Fill out and Mail to:	HoundHut Press
	P.O. Box 20062
	San Jose, CA 95160-0062
Or Fax to:	408-226-6160

Check One:

❏ New Addition ❏ Change Listing

Check One:

❏ Humane Society ❏ Breed Rescue Group

❏ Private Dog Rescue Group

❏ Other (please describe) _____

Name: _____

Address:_____

Address 2: _____

City: _____

State: _____ ZIP Code: _____

Phone: _____

FAX: _____

Website Address: _____

PLEASE CIRCLE YOUR ANSWER:

Do you have a kennel on-site?	YES	NO	
What animals do your adopt out?	DOGS	CATS	OTHER
Do you offer spay/neuter services?	YES	NO	
Do you offer on-site grooming?	YES	NO	
Do you offer on-site boarding?	YES	NO	
Do you offer low-cost,			
routine vaccinations?	YES	NO	

Order Form

SEND A COPY TO A FRIEND!

I want to order "Rescue Rover! 101 Ways You Can Help Abandoned Dogs" ($16.95)

For personal check, cashiers check and money orders, please Fill out and Mail to: HoundHut Press
P.O. Box 20062
San Jose, CA 95160-0062

CA State Addresses ONLY:

Rescue Rover $16.95
Shipping $3.95
Sales Tax (CA state residents only) .... +$1.40
CA TOTAL: $22.30

All other addresses:

Rescue Rover $16.95
Shipping $3.95
TOTAL: $20.90

For credit card orders, call 1-800-431-1579 or go to our website at www.houndhut.com for online, secure ordering.

Please have the following information ready:
Name: _____
Address:_____
Address 2: _____
City: _____
State: _____   ZIP Code: _____

Part 6:

About the Author

About the Author

ABOUT THE AUTHOR

Marie K. Whelan is active in Greyhound Friends for Life greyhound rescue, CARE - Companion Animal Rescue Effort, and the Greyhound Protection Alliance. She is a member of the Humane Society of the United States and the American Society for the Prevention of Cruelty to Animals. She lives in the San Francisco Bay Area with her family and three rescued dogs.

Printed in the United States
31788LVS00002B/226-228